the KILLERS

THE COMPLETE CHORD SONGBOOK

Published by
Wise Publications
14-15 Berners Street, London W1T 3LJ, UK.

Exclusive distributors:
Music Sales Limited,
Distribution Centre, Newmarket Road,
Bury St Edmunds, Suffolk IP33 3YB, UK.
Music Sales Pty Limited
120 Rothschild Avenue, Rosebery,
NSW 2018, Australia.

Order No. AM999559
ISBN 978-1-84938-398-1

Compiled by Nick Crispin.
Arranged by Matt Cowe.
Music processed by Paul Ewers Music Design.
Edited by Adrian Hopkins.

Printed in the EU.

www.musicsales.com

WISE PUBLICATIONS
part of The Music Sales Group
London/New York/Paris/Sydney/Copenhagen/Berlin/Madrid/Tokyo

SELECTED UK DISCOGRAPHY
ALBUMS

Sam's Town
(02/10/2006)
Vertigo CD 1706722

Sam's Town/Enterlude/When You
Were Young/Bling (Confession Of
A King)/For Reasons Unknown/
Read My Mind/Uncle Jonny/
Bones/ My List/This River Is Wild/
Why Do I Keep Counting?/ Exitlude/
Where The White Boys Dance

Hot Fuss
(07/07/2004)
Lizard King CD LIZARD011

Jenny Was A Friend Of Mine/
Mr. Brightside/Smile Like You Mean It/
Somebody Told Me/All These Things
That I've Done/Andy, You're A Star/
On Top/ Glamorous Indie Rock &
Roll/Believe Me Natalie/ Midnight
Show/Everything Will Be Alright

Sawdust
(12/11/2007)
Vertigo CD 1753374

Tranquilize [feat. Lou Reed]/
Shadowplay/All The Pretty Faces/
Leave The Bourbon On The Shelf/
Sweet Talk/Under The Gun/Where
The White Boys Dance/Show You
How/Move Away/ Glamorous Indie
Rock And Roll/ Who Let You Go?/
The Ballad Of Michael Valentine/
Ruby, Don't Take Your Love To Town/
Daddy's Eyes/Sam's Town [Abbey
Road Version]/Romeo And Juliet/
Change Your Mind/Mr. Brightside
[Jacques Lu Cont's Thin White
Duke Remix]

Day & Age
(24/11/2008)
Vertigo CD 1785121

Losing Touch/Human/Spaceman/
Joy Ride/A Dustland Fairytale/This Is
Your Life/I Can't Stay/Neon Tiger/
The World We Live In/Goodnight,
Travel Well/A Crippling Blow

Somebody Told Me
(15/03/2004)
7" (Lizard King LIZARD009X)
Somebody Told Me/
The Ballad Of Michael Valentine
CD (Lizard King LIZARD009)
Somebody Told Me/
The Ballad Of Michael Valentine/
Under The Gun

All These Things That I've Done
(30/08/2004)
7" (Lizard King LIZARD012X)
All These Things That I've Done/
Andy, You're A Star (Radio 1 Session)
CD (Lizard King LIZARD012)
All These Things That I've Done/
Why Don't You Find Out For
Yourself (Radio 1 Session)/
All These Things That I've Done
(Radio Edit)/All These Things That
I've Done (video)

Smile Like You Mean It
(02/05/2005)
7" (Lizard King LIZARD015X)
Smile Like You Mean It/
Ruby, Don't Take Your Love
To Town (Radio 1 Session)
CD (Lizard King LIZARD015)
Smile Like You Mean It/Get Trashed

SELECTED UK DISCOGRAPHY
SINGLES

Mr Brightside
(24/05/2004)
7" (Lizard King LIZARD010X)
Mr Brightside/Who Let You Go
CD1 (Lizard King LIZARD010CD1)
Mr Brightside/Change Your Mind
CD2 (Lizard King LIZARD010CD2)
Mr Brightside (Album Version)/
Somebody Told Me (Insider Remix)/
Midnight Show (SBN Live Session)/
Mr Brightside (Video)

Somebody Told Me
(Re-release: 10/01/2005)
CD1 (Lizard King LIZARD014CD1)
Somebody Told Me/Show You How
CD2 (Lizard King LIZARD014CD2)
Somebody Told Me/
Somebody Told Me (Mylo Mix)/
Somebody Told Me
(King Unique Vocal Mix)/
U-MYX Enhanced Section

When You Were Young
(18/09/2006)
7" (Vertigo 1706721)
When You Were Young/
Where The White Boys Dance
CD (Vertigo 1707658)
When You Were Young/
All The Pretty Faces

Bones (27/11/2006)
7" (Vertigo 1717120)
Bones/Daddy's Eyes
CD (Vertigo 1717078)
Bones/Daddy's Eyes

A Great Big Sled (05/12/2006)
Download Only Christmas Single

Read My Mind (26/02/2007)
7" (Vertigo 1724568)
Read My Mind/Read My Mind
(Steve Bays Remix)
CD (Vertigo 1724567)
Read My Mind/Read My Mind
(Pet Shop Boys
Stars Are Blazing Mix)

For Reasons Unknown
(25/06/2007)
7" (Vertigo 1736031)
For Reasons Unknown/Sam's Town
(Live From Abbey Road)
CD (Vertigo 1736030)
For Reasons Unknown/
Romeo And Juliet
(Live From Abbey Road)

Tranquillze
(5/11/2007)
7" (Vertigo 1753071)
Tranquilize [feat. Lou Reed]

Don't Shoot Me Santa
(27/11/2007)
Download Only Christmas Single

Human
(10/11/2008)
7" (Vertigo 1789799)
Human/A Crippling Blow

Spaceman
(09/02/2009)
7" (Vertigo 1797986)
Spaceman/Tidal Wave

Joseph, Better You Than Me
[feat. Elton John & Neil Tennant]
(16/12/2008)
Download Only Christmas Single

The World We Live In
(18/05/2009)
7" (Vertigo 2707364)
The World We Live In

A Dustland Fairytale
(10/08/2009)
7" (Vertigo 2714744)
A Dustland Fairytale/
Forget About What I Said

the **KILLERS**
SELECTED UK DISCOGRAPHY
SOUNDTRACKS

Spider-Man 3
(30/04/2007)
CD (Warner Music 9362499791)
Move Away

The Twilight Saga: New Moon
(19/10/2009)
CD (Atlantic 7567895625)
A White Demon Love Song

All The Pretty Faces

Words & Music by
Brandon Flowers, Dave Keuning, Mark Stoermer & Ronnie Vannucci

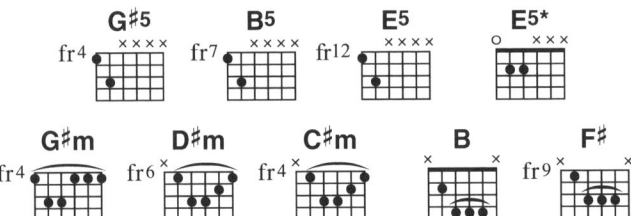

Tune guitar down a semitone

Intro

‖: G♯5 B5 | E5   G♯5 B5 | E5* :‖

‖: E5* B5 | G♯5   E5* B5 | G♯5 :‖

G♯m   D♯m
   Help me out, I need it,

                              C♯m D♯m
I don't feel like loving you no more.

                                 G♯m B5 E5   G♯5 B5 E5*
I don't feel like loving you no more.

| G♯5 B5 | E5   G♯5 B5 | E5 ‖

     G♯5   B5   E5   G♯5
Verse 1   Help me out, I need it,

        B5   E5*   G♯5
I don't feel like touching her no more.

        B5   E5
Help me out, I need it,

        G♯5   B5   E5*
I said I don't feel like touching her no more.

     E5*   B5   G♯5
Pre-chorus 1   Well how did it happen?

       E5*   B5   G♯5   E5*
I spent two long years in a strange strange land.

       B5   G♯5
Well how did it happen?

       E5*   B5   G♯5
I'd do any - thing just to be your man.

Chorus 1

    B   C♯m   D♯m

You're not going anywhere with - out me.

      F♯   G♯m

These trials don't prepare the air and no,

                   C♯m   D♯m

You're not telling anyone a - bout me.

         F♯

And you shake and you bleed while I sing my song.

Link 1

G♯5   B5   E5   G♯5   B5   E5*

I don't feel like, I don't feel like, I don't feel like loving you.

G♯5   B5   E5   G♯5   B5   E5*

I don't feel like, I don't feel like, I don't feel like loving you.

Verse 2

G♯5   B5   E5   G♯5   B5   E5*

All the different places   ringing out like a shotgun in my head.

G♯5   B5   E5   G♯5   B5   E5*

All the pretty faces   ringing out and I just can't go to bed.

Pre-chorus 2

       B5   G♯5

Well how did it happen?

         E5*   B5   G♯5   E5*

I spent two long years in a strange strange land.

       B5   G♯5

Well how did it happen?

     E5*   B5   G♯5

I'd do any - thing just to be your man.

     E5*   B5   G♯5

I'd do any - thing just to be your man.

Chorus 2   As Chorus 1

Bridge | G♯m | G♯m |

C♯m   D♯m

  I don't feel like touching you.

                                    F♯ G♯m

I don't feel like touching you.

                              C♯m

I don't feel like touching you.

                              D♯m

I don't feel like touching you.

                  F♯

You can't tell anyone a - bout me.

Chorus 3

B   C♯m   D♯m   F♯

You're not going any - where with - out me,

                      G♯m   C♯m

Help me out I need it.

                   D♯m   F♯

You can't tell anyone a - bout me,

Help me out I need it.

Link 2

‖: G♯5   B5 | E5 | G♯5   B5 | E5*   :‖

Outro

G♯5   B5   E5   G♯5   B5   E5*

I don't feel like, I don't feel like, I don't feel like loving you.

G♯5   B5   E5   G♯5   B5   E5*

I don't feel like, I don't feel like, I don't feel like loving you.

All These Things That I've Done

Words & Music by
Brandon Flowers, Dave Keuning, Mark Stoermer & Ronnie Vannucci

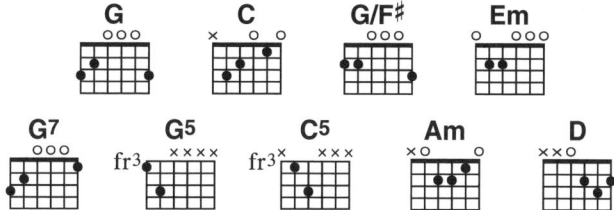

Tune guitar down a semitone

Intro

    G
When there's nowhere else to run,

           C
Is there room for one more son?

      G   **G/F♯**
One more son.

      Em
If you can hold on,

  C
If you can hold on, hold on.

Verse 1

  G
    I wanna stand up, I wanna let go,

You know, you know, no you don't, you don't.
C   **G**
    I wanna shine on in the hearts of men,

I want a meaning from the back of my broken hand.

Verse 2   Another head aches, another heart breaks,

I'm so much older than I can take.
C   **G**
    And my affection, well it comes and goes,

I need direction to perfection, no, no, no, no.

Chorus 1   Help me out.

Yeah, you know you got to help me out.
                                         C
Yeah, oh don't you put me on the backburner.
                              G
You know you got to help me out, yeah.

Verse 3   And when there's nowhere else to run,
G⁷
   Is there room for one more son?
       C
These changes ain't changing me,
     G
The cold-hearted boy I used to be.

Chorus 2   Yeah, you know you got to help me out,
                                    C
Yeah, oh don't you put me on the backburner,
                              G
You know you got to help me out, yeah.
                       Em
You're gonna bring yourself down,
                                  C
Yeah, you're gonna bring yourself down,
                                  G
Yeah, you're gonna bring yourself down.

Link 1 | **G⁵** | **G⁵** | **G⁵** | **G⁵**   ‖

G⁵
Bridge   I got soul, but I'm not a soldier.

I got soul, but I'm not a soldier.
C⁵
   I got soul, but I'm not a soldier.
G⁵
   I got soul, but I'm not a soldier.

I got soul, but I'm not a soldier.

I got soul, but I'm not a soldier.

Bridge (cont.)

C5
    I got soul, but I'm not a soldier.

G5
    I got soul, but I'm not a soldier.

Em
    I got soul, but I'm not a soldier.

C
    I got soul, but I'm not a soldier.

Link 2
   | G | G | G | G   ‖

Chorus 3

G
    Yeah, you know you got to help me out,

                                 C
Yeah, oh don't you put me on the backburner,

                      G
You know you got to help me out, yeah.

You're gonna bring yourself down,

Yeah, you're gonna bring yourself down.

                             C
Yeah, oh don't you put me on the backburner,

                     G
You're gonna bring yourself down,

                             Em
Yeah, you're gonna bring yourself down.

Outro

              Am   C
Over and in,   last call for sin.

                               D
While ev'ryone's lost, the battle is won,

                     G
With all these things that I've done.

                    Em
All these things that I've done.

           C
If you can hold on,

           D
If you can hold on.

   | G | G | G | G |

   | G | G | G | G   ‖

Andy, You're A Star

Words & Music by
Brandon Flowers, Dave Keuning, Mark Stoermer & Ronnie Vannucci

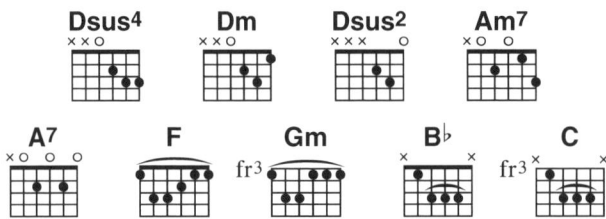

Tune guitar down a semitone

Intro

‖: Dsus⁴ | Dm Dsus² Dsus⁴ | Dsus⁴ Dm Dsus² |

| Dsus⁴ Dm Dsus² | Am⁷ | A⁷ Dsus⁴ |

| Dsus⁴ Dm Dsus² | Dsus⁴ Dm Dsus² :‖

2° (On the)

Verse 1

Dm Dsus² Dsus⁴   Dm   Dsus² Dsus⁴
On the   field   I re - member you   were

        Dm   Dsus² Dsus⁴
In - cre - di - ble,

Dm Dsus² Am⁷   A⁷   Dsus⁴ Dm Dsus² Dsus⁴
Hey shut   up,   hey shut up,   yeah.

Dm Dsus² Dsus⁴   Dm   Dsus² Dsus⁴
On the   field   I re - member you   were

        Dm   Dsus² Dsus⁴
In - cre - di - ble,

Dm Dsus² Am⁷   A⁷   Dsus⁴ Dm Dsus² Dsus⁴
Hey shut   up,   hey shut up,   yeah.

Dm Dsus² F   Gm   Dm
On the   mats with the boys, you think you're alone,

      F   Gm   Dm
With the pain that you drain from love.

    F   B♭   Gm   C
In a car with a girl, pro - mise me she's not your world,

            Dsus⁴
'Cause Andy, you're a star.

Link 1

| Dsus4 | Dm Dsus2 Dsus4 | Dsus4 Dm Dsus2 |
(star.)

| Dsus4 Dm Dsus2 | Dsus4 | Dm Dsus2 Dsus4 |

| Dsus4 Dm Dsus2 | Dsus4 Dm Dsus2 ‖
(Leave your)

Verse 2

Dm   Dsus2 Dsus4   Dm   Dsus2
Leave your   number on the locker and

Dsus4 Dm Dsus2 Dsus4
I'll give you a   call,

Dm Dsus2 Am7   A7 Dsus4 Dm Dsus2 Dsus4
Hey shut   up, hey shut up, yeah.

Dm   Dsus2 Dsus4 Dm   Dsus2 Dsus4
Leave your   legacy in gold on the   plaques

        Dm Dsus2 Dsus4
That line the   hall,

Dm Dsus2 Am7   A7 Dsus4 Dm Dsus2 Dsus4
Hey shut   up, hey shut up, yeah.

Dm Dsus2 F   Gm   Dm
On the   streets, such a sweet face jumpin' town,

        F   Gm   Dm
In the staff room the verdict is in.

       F   Bb   Gm   C
In a car with a girl, pro - mise me she's not your world,

Chorus

                   F
'Cause Andy, you're a star.

        Bb
In nobody's eyes but mine.

          F
Andy, you're a star.

        Bb
In nobody's eyes but mine.

          Dm
Andy, you're a star.

        Bb   C   Dsus4
In nobody's eyes, in nobody's eyes but mine.

Outro

‖: Dsus4 | Dm Dsus2 Dsus4 | Dsus4 Dm Dsus2 |
(mine)

| Dsus4 Dm Dsus2 | Am7 | A7 | Dsus4 |

| Dsus4 Dm Dsus2 | Dsus4 Dm Dsus2 :‖

| Dsus4 | Dm Dsus2 Dsus4 | Dsus4 Dm Dsus2 |

| Dsus4 Dm Dsus2 | Am7 | Am7 | ‖

17

The Ballad Of Michael Valentine

Words & Music by
Brandon Flowers, Dave Keuning, Mark Stoermer & Ronnie Vannucci

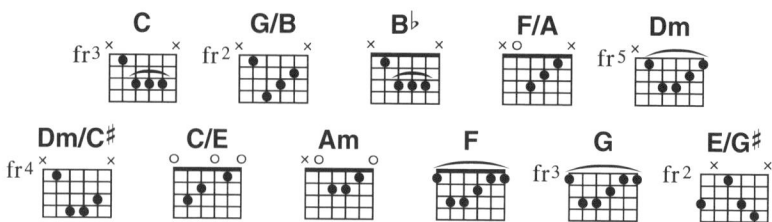

Intro

    C   G/B   B♭
Michael plays with stars,

            F/A   Dm   Dm/C♯
Soul sister won't you take a ride in his car?

      C   G/B   C
Late to call, when you wanted to be all.

            G/B   B♭
Baby, baby don't be so shy,

         F/A   Dm   Dm/C♯
Rock children hold your heads up high in the night,

      C   G/B   C
While I try and tell the ballad of Valen - tine.

Link

You got it bad, but you know it's true,

Verse 1

I caught up with a friend in Dallas.

  C/E
We took a trip to New Orleans,

    Am   F   G
Those black-eyed ladies won't say they're sorry.

  C
We finally caught a train to Memphis,

    C/E
Where everybody talks the same.

    Am   F   G
Those blue suede babies all know my name.

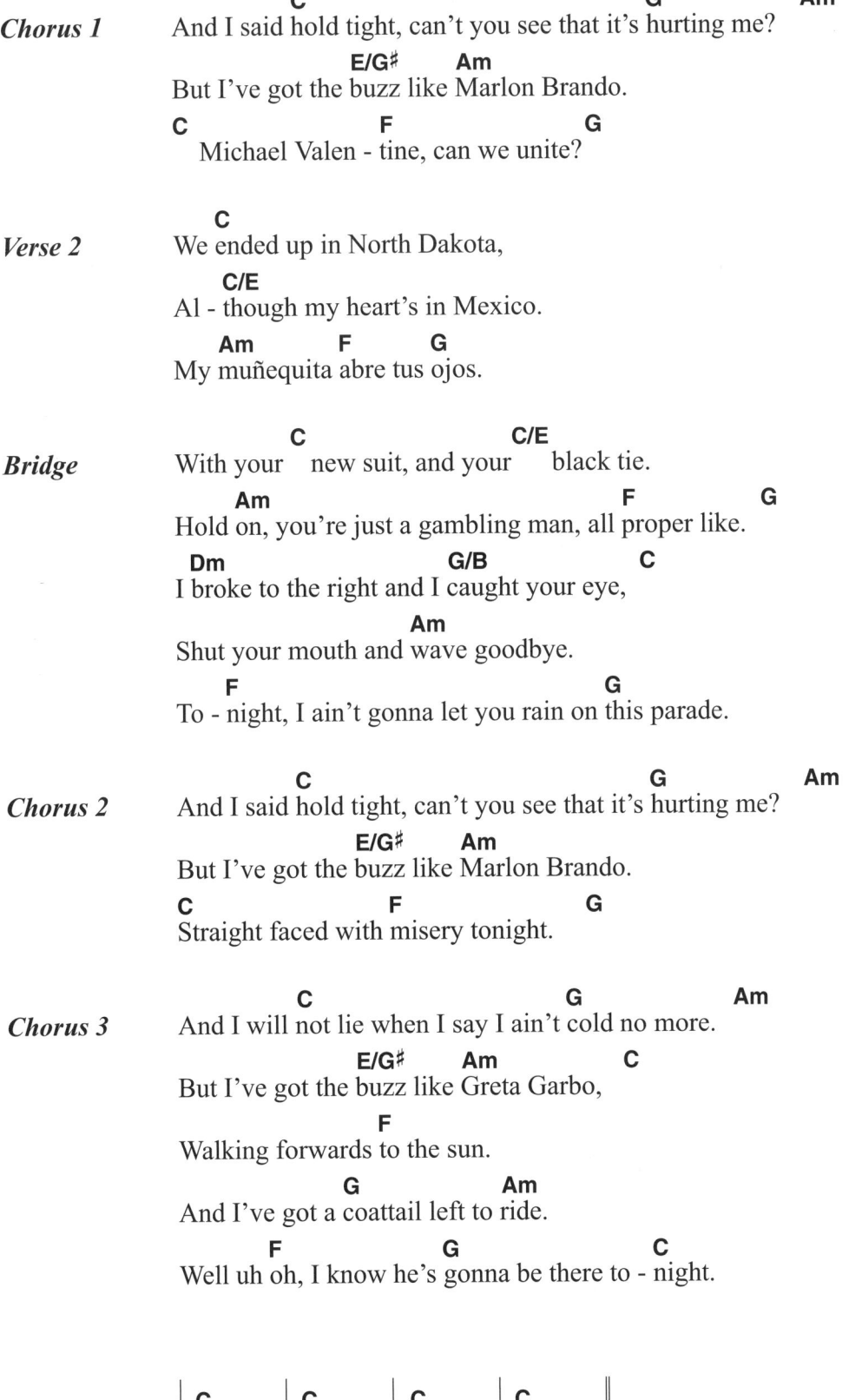

Chorus 1

         C   G   Am

And I said hold tight, can't you see that it's hurting me?

                   E/G♯   Am

But I've got the buzz like Marlon Brando.

C   F   G

    Michael Valen - tine, can we unite?

Verse 2

           C

We ended up in North Dakota,

           C/E

Al - though my heart's in Mexico.

       Am   F   G

My muñequita abre tus ojos.

Bridge

                 C   C/E

With your   new suit, and your   black tie.

            Am   F   G

Hold on, you're just a gambling man, all proper like.

    Dm   G/B   C

I broke to the right and I caught your eye,

                               Am

Shut your mouth and wave goodbye.

       F   G

To - night, I ain't gonna let you rain on this parade.

Chorus 2

         C   G   Am

And I said hold tight, can't you see that it's hurting me?

                   E/G♯   Am

But I've got the buzz like Marlon Brando.

C   F   G

Straight faced with misery tonight.

Chorus 3

         C   G   Am

And I will not lie when I say I ain't cold no more.

                   E/G♯   Am   C

But I've got the buzz like Greta Garbo,

                   F

Walking forwards to the sun.

                   G   Am

And I've got a coattail left to ride.

       F   G   C

Well uh oh, I know he's gonna be there to - night.

| C | C | C | C |

Believe Me Natalie

Words & Music by
Brandon Flowers, Dave Keuning, Mark Stoermer & Ronnie Vannucci

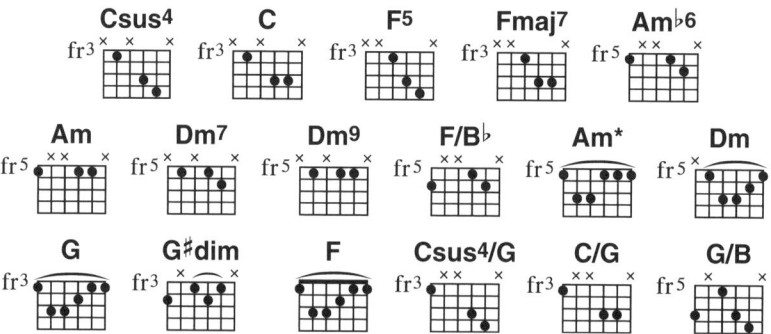

Intro

Ad lib. keyboard   Drums
                               4

| Csus⁴ C | Csus⁴ C | F5 Fmaj⁷ | F5 Fmaj⁷ |
| F5 Fmaj⁷ | Am♭6 Am | Dm⁷ Dm⁹ | Dm⁷ Dm⁹ |

(Be-)

Verse 1

      Csus⁴   C   Csus⁴ C   F5   Fmaj⁷ F5
Be - lieve me, Natalie, listen   Natalie, this is

    Fmaj⁷   F5   Fmaj⁷ Am♭6   Am   Dm⁷   Dm⁹ Dm⁷
Your last chance to find a go-go   dance to disco   now.

Dm⁹   Csus⁴   C   Csus⁴ C   F5   Fmaj⁷ F5
Please be - lieve me, Natalie, listen   Natalie, this is

     N.C.   F5   Fmaj⁷ Am♭6   Am Dm⁷   Dm⁹ Dm⁷
Your last chance to find a go-go dance to disco now.

      Dm⁹   F5   Fmaj⁷ Am♭6   Am   Dm⁷   Dm⁹ Dm
For - get what they said in Soho, leave the oh-no's out.

Dm⁹   F/B♭   F5   Fmaj⁷ F5
And be - lieve me, Natalie, listen Natalie, this is

Fmaj⁷ N.C.
Your   last chance.

Link 1   ‖: **F5** **Fmaj7** | **Am♭6** **Am** | **Dm7** **Dm9** | **Dm7** **Dm9** :‖

Verse 2

       Csus4 **C**   **Csus4** **C**   **F5**   **Fmaj7** **F5**
There is an   old cliché under your Monet, baby.

    Fmaj7   **F5**   **Fmaj7**
Re - member the arch of roses,

Am♭6   **Am**   **Dm7**   **Dm9** **Dm7**
Right a - bove your couch.

    Dm9   **F5**   **Fmaj7**
For - get what they said in Soho,

Am♭6   **Am**   **Dm7**   **Dm9** **Dm7**
Leave the oh-no's out.

Dm9   **F/B♭**   **Am***
Yes, there is an old cliché under your Monet, baby.

Bridge

    Dm
You left the station now to the floor,

    Am*
With speculation, what was it for?

   Dm   **G**
In that old hallway, Mom says why don't you stay?

        G♯dim   **Am Am♭6**
You've been a - way for a long time.

Verse 3

   G   **F**
Be - lieve me, Natalie, this is

        F5   **Fmaj7**   **Am♭6 Am Dm7 Dm9 Dm7**
Your last chance to find a go-go.

   Dm9   **F5**   **Fmaj7**   **Am♭6 Am Dm7 Dm9 Dm7**
For - get what they said in Soho,

Dm9 F5   **Fmaj7 Am♭6 Am**
And walk a - way.

    Dm7   **Dm9**   **Dm7**
If my dreams for us can't get you

Dm9   **Csus4** **C** **Csus4**
Through just one more day,

    C   **Csus4/G C/G Csus4/G C/G**
It's al - right by me.

Outro

      F5   **Fmaj7**   **Am♭6 Am**
God help me somehow.

        Dm7   **Dm9**   **Dm7 Dm9**
There's no time for sur - vival left,

     Csus4 C   **Csus4**
The time is now.

       C   **Csus4/G C/G G♯dim**   **Am G/B**
'Cause this might be   your last chance

    C   **Am**
To disco, oh, oh.

| **Csus4 C** | **Csus4 C** | **Am♭6 Am** | **Am♭6 Am** |

| **Csus4/G C/G** | **F5 Fmaj7** | **F/B♭** |

Bling (Confession Of A King)

Words & Music by
Brandon Flowers, Dave Keuning, Mark Stoermer & Ronnie Vannucci

F#   Bm   G   Em   A   Em9   F#m   D

Intro | F# |

Chorus 1

Bm   G
   When I offer you survival,
                                          Em
You say it's hard enough to live.
                          G   A
It's not so bad, it's not so bad,
                 Em9   G   A
How do you know that you're right?

Verse 1

          Bm
I a - woke on the roadside,
     G
In the land of the free ride,
     Em
I can't pull it any longer,
          Bm
And the sun is beating down my neck.

So I ran with the devil,
     G
Left a trail of excuses.
     Em
Like a stone on the water,
     Bm
The elements decide my fate.
          G A
Watch it go,   bling.

Chorus 2

```
       Bm                           F♯m     G
          When I offer you sur - vival,

                                         A
          You say it's hard enough to live.
                      F♯m
          Don't tell me that it's over,
                 G                              A
          Stand up, poor and tired, but more than this.
                       F♯m
          How do you know that you're right
                     G                    A
          If you're not nervous anymore?
                    F♯m           G
          It's not so bad, it's not so bad.
```

Verse 2

```
                            Bm
          I feel my vision slipping in and out of focus,
                      G
          But I'm pushing on for that horizon.
                      Em
          I'm pushing on,
                      Bm
          Now I've got that blowing wind against my face.

          So you sling rocks at the rip tide,
                 G
          Am I wrong or am I right?
                    Em
          I hit the bottom with a "huh!"
                             Bm
          Quite strange, I get my glory in the desert rain.
                        G  A
          Watch it go,     bling.
```

Chorus 3

Bm   F♯m   G
When I offer you sur - vival,

                               A
You say it's hard enough to live.

                    F♯m
And I'll tell you when it's over,

       G   A
Shut up, poor and tired but more than this.

                 F♯m
How do you know that you're right,

           G   A
If you're not nervous anymore?

          F♯m   G
It's not so bad, it's not so bad.

Bridge

‖: D
Higher and higher,

We're gonna take it down to the wire,

                 G   A   Bm F♯m
We're gonna make it out of the fire,

G   A
Higher and higher. :‖

D
Higher and higher,

                 G
We're gonna take it down to the wire,

                   A   Bm F♯m
We're gonna make it out oh,_____

G   A   D
Higher and higher.

Outro

G   A   Bm
It ain't hard to hold,

         F♯m   G
When it shines like gold,

             A   D
You'll re - member me.

Change Your Mind

Words & Music by
Brandon Flowers, Dave Keuning, Mark Stoermer & Ronnie Vannucci

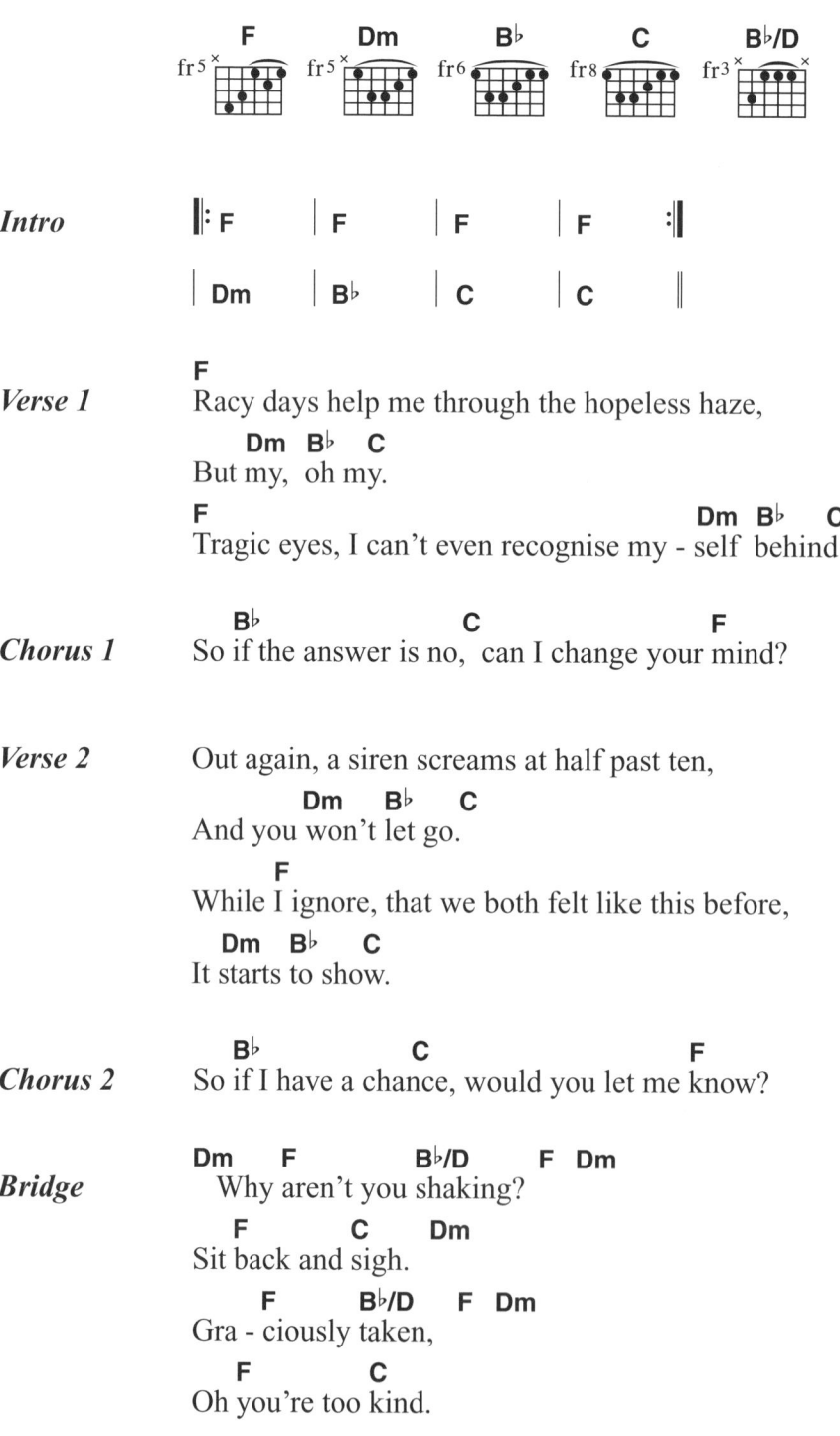

Intro   ‖: F | F | F | F :‖

| Dm | B♭ | C | C ‖

Verse 1

F
Racy days help me through the hopeless haze,
    Dm B♭ C
But my, oh my.
F
Tragic eyes, I can't even recognise my - self behind.
    Dm B♭   C

Chorus 1

    B♭   C   F
So if the answer is no, can I change your mind?

Verse 2

Out again, a siren screams at half past ten,
    Dm B♭ C
And you won't let go.
    F
While I ignore, that we both felt like this before,
Dm B♭ C
It starts to show.

Chorus 2

    B♭   C   F
So if I have a chance, would you let me know?

Bridge

Dm   F   B♭/D   F Dm
  Why aren't you shaking?
    F   C   Dm
Sit back and sigh.
     F   B♭/D   F Dm
Gra - ciously taken,
    F   C
Oh you're too kind.

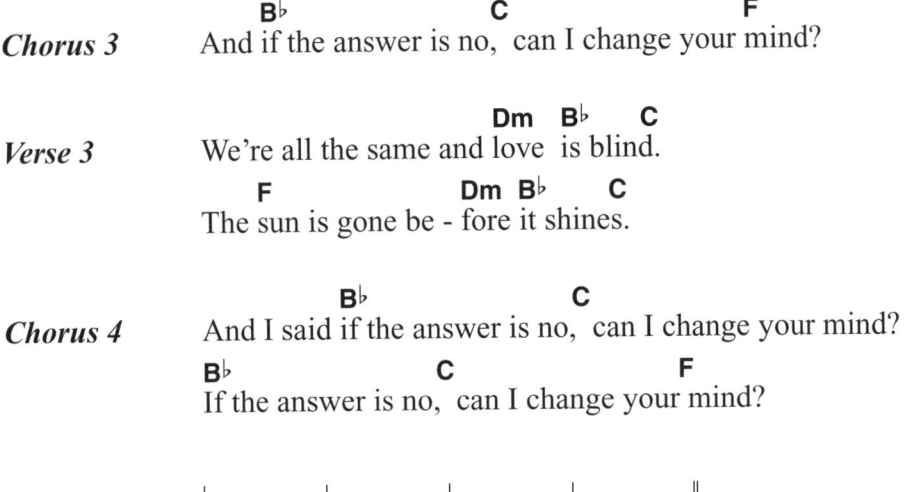

Chorus 3
        B♭   C   F
And if the answer is no, can I change your mind?

Verse 3
                                  Dm B♭   C
We're all the same and love is blind.
              F   Dm B♭   C
The sun is gone be - fore it shines.

Chorus 4
                  B♭   C
And I said if the answer is no, can I change your mind?
B♭   C   F
If the answer is no, can I change your mind?

Outro | F | F | F | F   ‖

A Crippling Blow

Words by Brandon Flowers
Music by Brandon Flowers, Dave Keuning, Mark Stoermer & Ronnie Vannucci

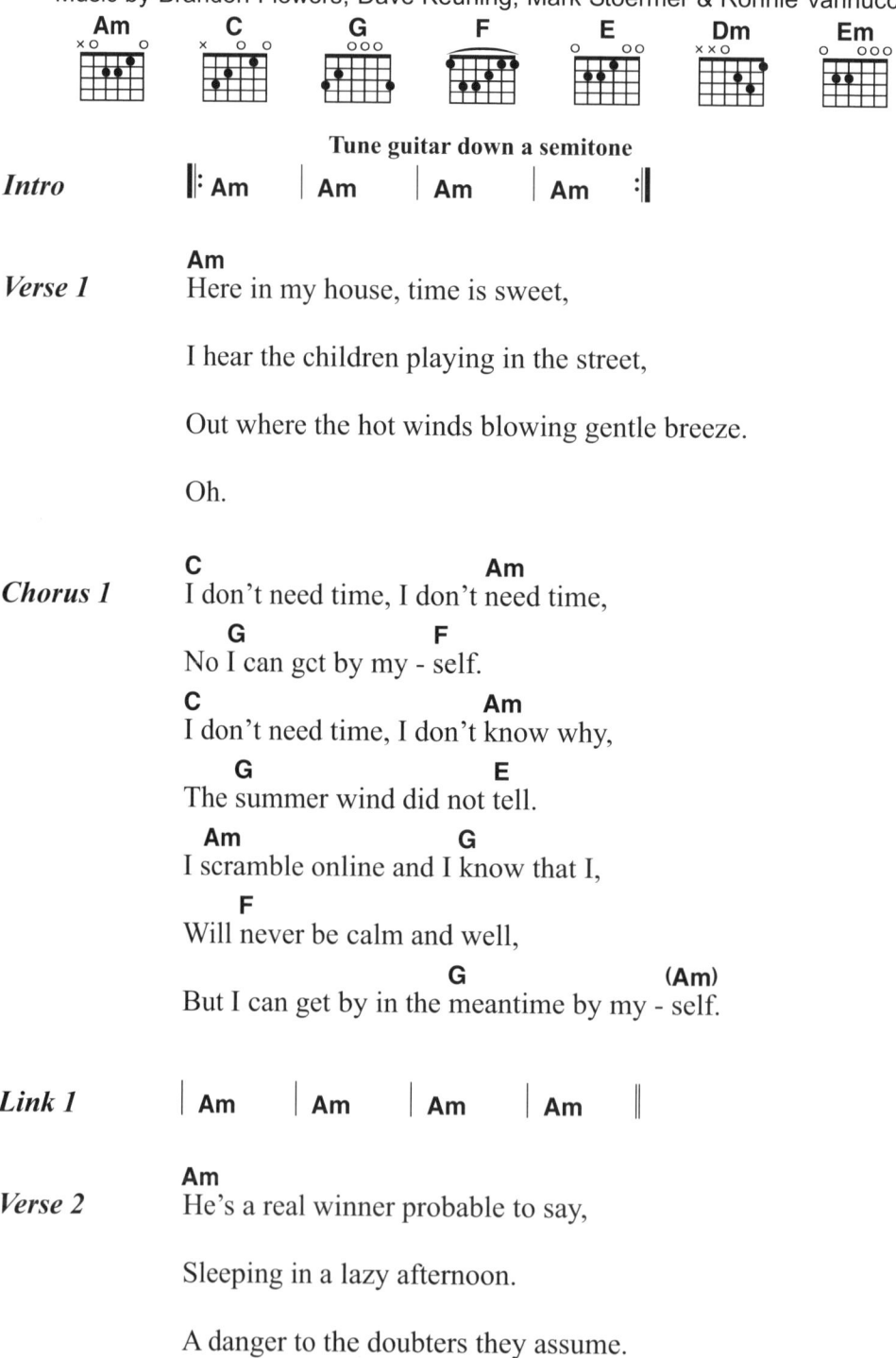

Tune guitar down a semitone

Intro   ‖: Am | Am | Am | Am :‖

Verse 1
Am
Here in my house, time is sweet,

I hear the children playing in the street,

Out where the hot winds blowing gentle breeze.

Oh.

Chorus 1
C   Am
I don't need time, I don't need time,
    G   F
No I can gct by my - self.
C   Am
I don't need time, I don't know why,
    G   E
The summer wind did not tell.
  Am   G
I scramble online and I know that I,
    F
Will never be calm and well,
                          G   (Am)
But I can get by in the meantime by my - self.

Link 1 | Am | Am | Am | Am ‖

Verse 2
Am
He's a real winner probable to say,

Sleeping in a lazy afternoon.

A danger to the doubters they assume.

Oh.

Chorus 2

    C   Am
I don't need time, I don't need time,

        G   F
No I can get by my - self.

    C   Am
I don't need time, I don't know why,

        G   E
The summer wind did not tell.

   Am   G
I scramble online and I know that I,

      F
Will never be calm and well,

               G   Am
But I can get by in the meantime by my - self.

Bridge

    Dm   Am E
Deal me a crippling blow.

    Dm   Am   E
Steal me from under my clothes,

        (Am)
A crippling blow.

Link 2 | Am | Am | Am | Am   ‖

Chorus 3

    C   Am
I don't need time, I don't need time,

        G   F
No I can get by my - self.

    C   Am
I don't need time, I don't know why,

        G   E
The summer wind did not tell.

   Am   G
I scramble online and I know that I,

      F
Will never be calm and well,

               G   Am
But I can get by in the meantime by my - self.

      F   G   Am Em
Lord, I can get by in the meantime by my - self.___

Outro |Dm | Em | Am | Em |

    Dm   Em   Am Em
I can get by in the meantime by my - self.

    |Dm | Em | Am | Em   ‖ *To fade*

Bones

Words & Music by
Brandon Flowers, Dave Keuning, Mark Stoermer & Ronnie Vannucci

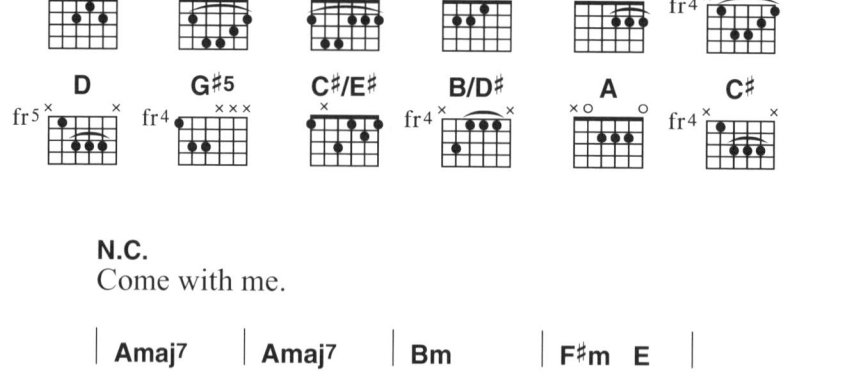

Intro

N.C.
Come with me.

| Amaj⁷ | Amaj⁷ | Bm | F♯m E |
| Dmaj⁷ | Dmaj⁷ | E | E |

(We took a)

Verse 1

E   C♯m   D
We took a back road, we're gonna look at the stars,

         Bm   C♯m
We took a back road in my car.

              F♯m   D
Down to the ocean, it's only water and sand,

           G♯5   C♯m
And in the ocean we'll hold hands.

                                         D   Bm
But I don't really like you, apolo - getically dressed in the best,

           C♯m
But on a heartbeat glide.

           F♯m   D
Without an answer, the thunder speaks for the sky,

           G♯5   C♯m   D
And on the cold, wet dirt I cry._____

           C♯m Bm A G♯5 F♯m   E
And on the cold, wet dirt I   cry.

Chorus 1

Amaj⁷
Don't you wanna come with me?
                              Bm   F♯m E   Dmaj⁷
Don't you wanna feel my bones on your bones?
                E
It's only natural.

Verse 2

                    C♯m   D   Bm   E   C♯/E♯
A cinematic vision en - sued   like the holiest dream.
          F♯m
Is someone calling?
      D
An angel whispers my name,
            G♯5   **C♯m   D**
But the message relayed is the same:
                              E
"Wait till tomorrow, you'll be fine."

But it's gone to the dogs in my mind.
  C♯m   D   Bm   C♯m   F♯m
I always hear them when the dead of night,
        D   G♯5   C♯m   D
Comes calling to save me from this fight.
              C♯m Bm A   G♯5 F♯m   E
But they can ne - ver   wrong this   right.

Chorus 2

                    Amaj⁷
Don't you wanna come with me?
                              Bm   F♯m E   Dmaj⁷
Don't you wanna feel my bones on your bones?
                E
It's only natural.
                    Amaj⁷
Don't you wanna swim with me?
                              Bm   F♯m E   Dmaj⁷
Don't you wanna feel my skin   on your skin?
                E
It's only natural.

Bridge

F#m   C#/E#
(Never had a lover), I never had a lover.

E   B/D#
(Never had soul), I never had soul.

A   C#
(Never had a good time), and I never had a good time.

D   E
(Never got gold), I never got gold.

Chorus 3

                Amaj⁷
Don't you wanna come with me?

                     Bm   F#m E   Dmaj⁷
Don't you wanna feel my bones on your bones?

        E
It's only natural.

               Amaj⁷
Don't you wanna swim with me?

                   Bm   F#m E   Dmaj⁷
Don't you wanna feel my skin   on your skin?

        E
It's only natural.

Chorus 4

                Amaj⁷   D
Don't you wanna come with me?

                   E   F#m E   Dmaj⁷
Don't you wanna feel my bones on your bones?

        E
It's only natural.

              Amaj⁷   D
Come and take a swim with me.

                   E   F#m E   Dmaj⁷
Don't you wanna feel my skin   on your skin?

        E   Amaj⁷
It's only natural.

Daddy's Eyes

Words & Music by
Brandon Flowers, Dave Keuning, Mark Stoermer & Ronnie Vannucci

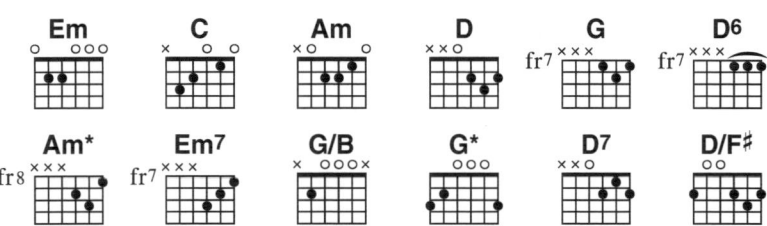

Verse 1

Em   C
I'll tell you what you wanna know,
                                    Am
But boy you better listen close.
                                Em
People gonna tell you lies,
    D   Em
Don't let it come as a surprise.

That woman's on my back again,
                              Am
I know she's got the best in - tentions.
                              Em
When you begin to realise,
    D   G
You know you got your daddy's eyes.

Pre-chorus 1

                                              D6
And there's something that I want to say,
          Am*
I love her too.
              Em7   D6
And all of this has got nothing to do with you.

Chorus 1

          Em   C
And I'd   like to stay but I can't be - cause,
                              Am
I've been fooling around and I know,
                                  Em
That you called because you never even knew,
                    D
That it was hurting me.

Verse 2

Em   C
When you put it on the other hand,

                                  Am
When you're old enough to understand.

                            Em
That glove will bring it all to life,

 D   Em
I didn't say that made it right.

                                C
'Cause that woman's on my back again,

                        Am
I know she's got the best in - tentions.

                        Em
When you begin to realise,

  D   G
You know you got your daddy's eyes.

                                      D6
Pre-chorus 2   And there's something that I want to say,

            Am*
I love her too.

                    Em7   D6
And all of this has got nothing to do with you.

                 Em   C
Chorus 2   And I'd   like to stay but I can't be - cause,

                        Am
I've been fooling around and I know,

                                  Em
That you called because you never even knew,

                  D
That it was hurting me.

            Em   C
And I'd   like to stay but I can't be - cause,

                        Am
I've been fooling around and I know,

                                  Em
That you called because you never even knew,

                  D
That it was hurting me.

Bridge

          C   G/B Am G*
Sometimes people get tired,

              C   G   D7
And I woke up a little too late to lie.

                 C   G/B Am G
Dreams should last a long time,

         C   G   D7
This is not what I'd call good - bye.

Solo   ‖: Em | C | Am | Em D :‖

Chorus 3

     Em   C
    I'd love to stay but I can't be - cause,

                      Am
I've been fooling around and I know,

                                    Em
That you called because you never even knew,

                   D
That it was hurting me.

        Em   C
And I   would love to stay but I can't be - cause,

                      Am
I've been fooling around and I know,

                                  Em
That you called because you never even knew,

                   D
That it was hurting me.

     Em   G   D/F♯
Me.

                  Am   G   D/F♯   Em
And I love her too.

Don't Shoot Me Santa

Words & Music by
Brandon Flowers, Dave Keuning, Mark Stoermer & Ronnie Vannucci

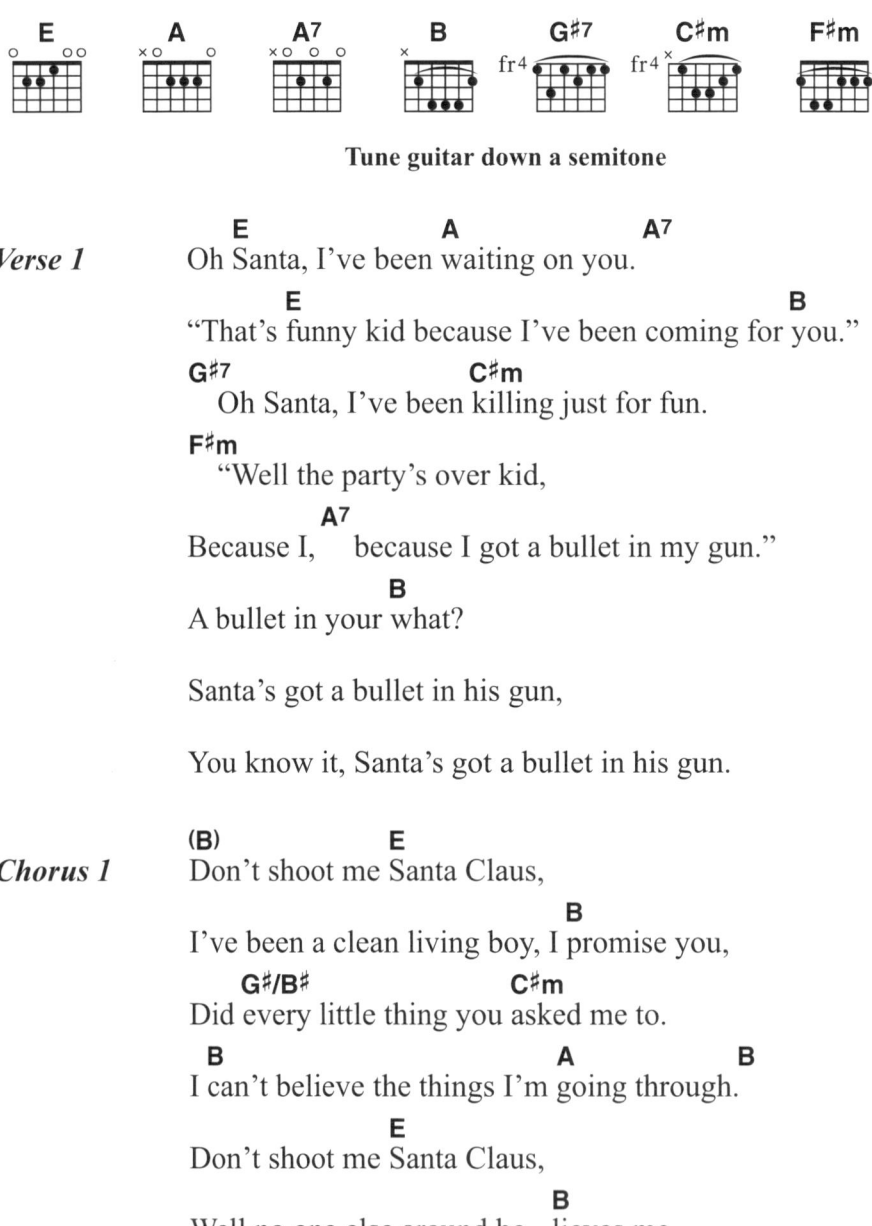

Tune guitar down a semitone

Verse 1

             E   A   A⁷
Oh Santa, I've been waiting on you.

        E   B
"That's funny kid because I've been coming for you."

G♯7   C♯m
  Oh Santa, I've been killing just for fun.

F♯m
   "Well the party's over kid,

          A⁷
Because I,   because I got a bullet in my gun."

                  B
A bullet in your what?

Santa's got a bullet in his gun,

You know it, Santa's got a bullet in his gun.

Chorus 1

           (B)   E
Don't shoot me Santa Claus,

                                 B
I've been a clean living boy, I promise you,

      G♯/B♯   C♯m
Did every little thing you asked me to.

     B   A   B
I can't believe the things I'm going through.

                 E
Don't shoot me Santa Claus,

                          B
Well no one else around be - lieves me,

        G♯/B♯   C♯m
But the children on the block they tease me,

     B   A   B
I couldn't let them off that easy.

Verse 2	E A A⁷

Verse 2

        E   **A**   **A⁷**
Oh Santa, it's been a   real hard year.

                    E
"There just ain't no gettin' around this,

                  B
Life is hard, but look at me,   I turned out all right."
G♯7   **C♯m**
   Hey Santa, why don't we talk about it,   work it out?
           F♯m
"Believe me, this ain't what I wanted,

I love all you kids, you know that.

      A⁷
Hell,   I remember when you were just ten years old,

Playing out there in the desert,
                  B
Just waiting for a sip of that sweet Mojave rain."

In the sweet Mojave rain,

The boy was on his own.

Chorus 2

  (B)   **E**
Don't shoot me Santa Claus,

                  B
I've been a clean living boy, I promise you,
    G♯/B♯   **C♯m**
Did every little thing you asked me to.
  B   **A**   **B**
I can't believe the things I'm going through.
    E
Hey, Santa Claus,

                  B
Well no one else around be - lieves me,
    G♯/B♯   **C♯m**
But the children on the block they tease me,
  B   **A**   **B**
I couldn't let them off that easy.

Bridge

    (B)   **A**
They had it coming,

        B
So why can't you see?

            E   **A**
I couldn't turn my cheek no longer.

F♯m   **C♯m**   **F♯m**
   The sun is going down and Christmas is near,

     B   **E**
Just look the other way and I'll disappear for - ever.

Whoo!

Guitar solo | **E** | **E** | **B** | **G♯/B♯** |

                 | **C♯m** | **B** | **A** | **B**   ‖

Chorus 3

    (B)   **E**
Don't shoot me Santa Claus,

                     B
Well no one else around be - lieves me,

        G♯/B♯   **C♯m**
But the children on the street they tease me,

  B   **A**
I couldn't let them off that easy.

      B
Be - lieve me,

E   **C♯m** **A** **B** **E**
Santa, Santa.

A Dustland Fairytale

Words by Brandon Flowers
Music by Brandon Flowers, Dave Keuning, Mark Stoermer & Ronnie Vannucci

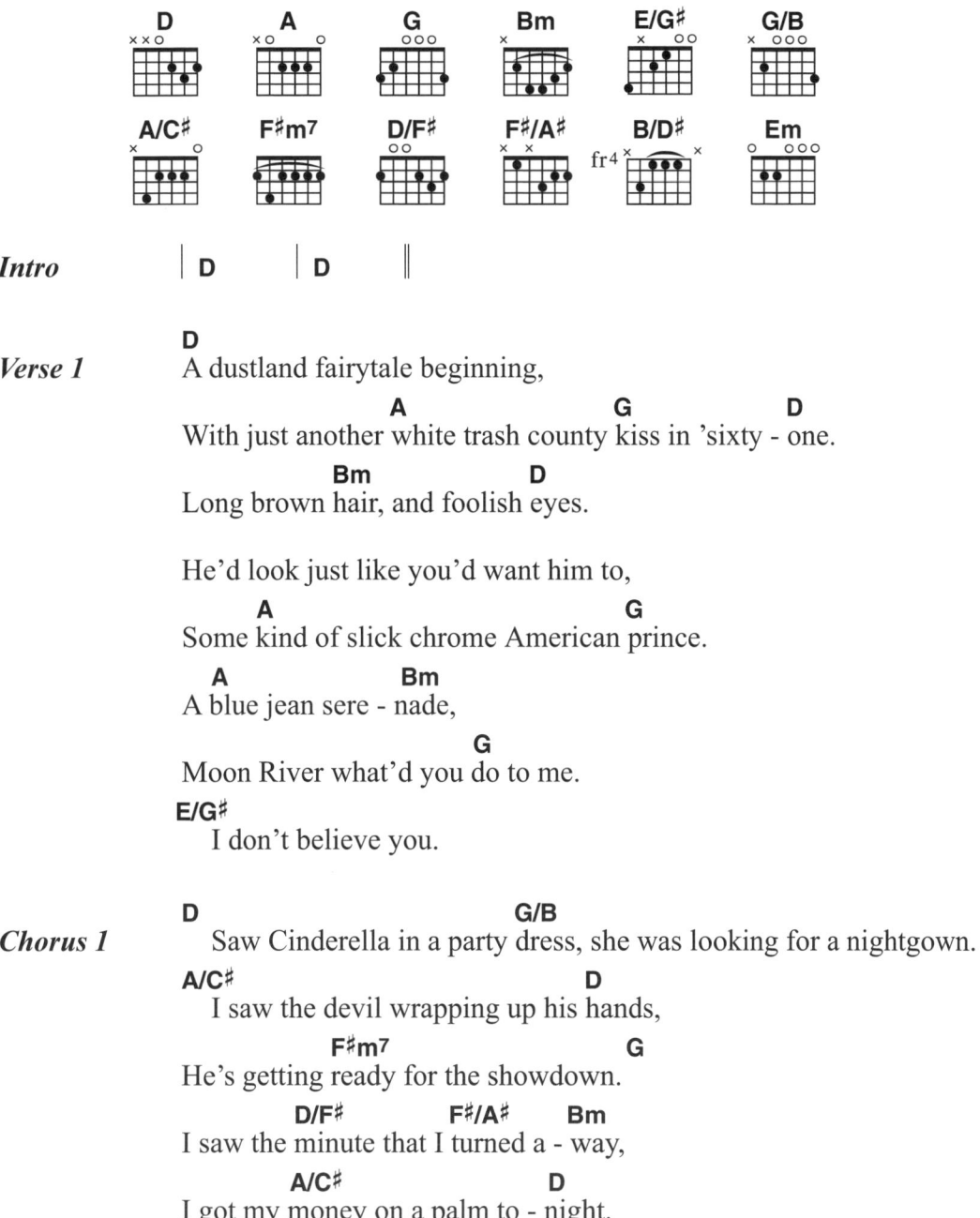

Intro | D | D   ‖

Verse 1

   D
A dustland fairytale beginning,
            A   **G**   **D**
With just another white trash county kiss in 'sixty - one.
     Bm   **D**
Long brown hair, and foolish eyes.

He'd look just like you'd want him to,
     A   **G**
Some kind of slick chrome American prince.
  A   **Bm**
A blue jean sere - nade,
            G
Moon River what'd you do to me.
E/G♯
I don't believe you.

Chorus 1

   D   **G/B**
Saw Cinderella in a party dress, she was looking for a nightgown.
A/C♯   **D**
I saw the devil wrapping up his hands,
      F♯m7   **G**
He's getting ready for the showdown.
     D/F♯   **F♯/A♯** **Bm**
I saw the minute that I turned a - way,
     A/C♯   **D**
I got my money on a palm to - night.

Verse 2

    D   A   G
Change came in disguise of reve - lation, set his soul on fire.

       A   Bm   D
She said she always knew he'd come a - round.

And the decades disappear,

              Bm
Like sinking ships but we persevere.

         G   Bm   G   D
God gives us hope but we still fear, what we don't know.

Your mind is poison.

Bm   G
   Castles in the sky, sit stranded, vandalized.

   E/G♯
My drawbridge is closing.

Chorus 2

    D   G/B
   Saw Cinderella in a party dress, but she was looking for a nightgown.

A/C♯   D
   I saw the devil wrapping up his hands,

              F♯m7
He's getting ready for the showdown.

G   D/F♯   F♯/A♯   Bm
   I saw the ending when they turned the page,

          A/C♯   D
I threw my money and I ran a - way,

             F♯m7   A
Straight to the valley of the great di - vide,

Bridge

   (A)   D
Out where the dreams are high.

               A   G
Out where the wind don't blow,

             F♯m7   Bm
Out here the good girls die.

          A   D
And the sky won't snow.

          A   G
Out here the bird don't sing,

             F♯m7   G
Out here the field don't grow.

            F♯m7   Bm
Out here the bell don't ring,

B/D♯   Em
   Out hear the bell don't ring,

G
   Out here the good girls die.

Chorus 3

    A   **Bm**
Now Cinderella don't you go to sleep,

It's such a bitter form of refuge.

A/C♯   **D**
Why don't you know the kingdom's under siege,

     F♯m7   **G**
And everybody needs you?

         D/F♯   **F♯/A♯**   **Bm**
Is there still magic in the midnight sun,

        A/C♯   **D**
Or did you leave it back in 'sixty - one?

      D/F♯   **G**
In the cadence of a young man's eyes,

            A   **D**
Out where the dreams are high.

Outro | **D** | **D** **A** | **G** | **G** **F♯m7**| **Bm** |

               | **A/C♯** | **D**   ‖ *Fade out*

Enterlude

Words & Music by
Brandon Flowers, Dave Keuning, Mark Stoermer & Ronnie Vannucci

Verse 1

     G♯m   B E
We hope you en - joy your stay,

    G♯m   F♯   E   B F♯/A♯
It's good to have you with us even if it's just for the day.

    G♯m   F♯   B E
We hope you en - joy your stay,

     G♯m   F♯
Out - side the sun is shining,

    E   B   F♯/A♯
It seems like heaven ain't far a - way.

    G♯m   F♯
It's good to have you with us,

    E   B   G♯m F♯ E
Even if it's just for the day.

Exitlude

Words & Music by
Brandon Flowers, Dave Keuning, Mark Stoermer & Ronnie Vannucci

Tune guitar down a semitone

Verse 1

      C   C/E   F   C
Aggressively   we all de - fend the role we play,

                  C/E   F   G   Am
Regrettably   the time's come to send you on your way.

                      G   F   C   G/B
We've seen it all;   bonfires of trust, flash floods of pain.

    Am   G   F
It doesn't really matter, don't you worry it'll all work out.

    Am   G   F
No it doesn't even matter, don't you worry that ain't what it's all a - bout.

Chorus 1

    Am   C   F
We hope you en - joyed your stay,

    Am   G   F   C   G/B
It's good to have you with us, even if it's just for the day.

    Am   G   C   F
We hope you en - joyed your stay,

        Am   G   F   C   G/B
Out - side the sun is shining, seems like heaven ain't far a - way.

    Am   G   F   G
It's good to have you with us,

                          C
Even if it's just for the day.

Interlude

| C | Am | G | F | |
(day)
| C | Am | G | F | ‖

Chorus 2

         C
‖: It's good to have you with us, even if it's just for the day.

Outside the sun is shining, seems like heaven ain't far away. :‖

Seems like heaven ain't far away.

Everything Will Be Alright

Words & Music by
Brandon Flowers, Dave Keuning, Mark Stoermer & Ronnie Vannucci

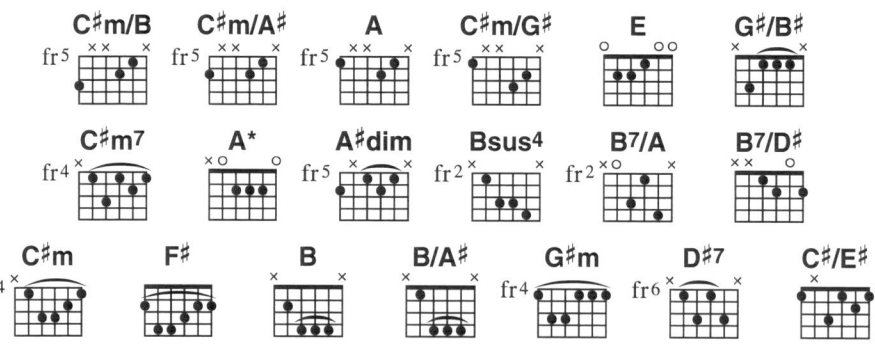

Tune guitar down a semitone

Intro
| C#m/B C#m/A# | A C#m/G# | | C#m/B C#m/A# | A C#m/G# |

Verse 1
```
        C#m/B     C#m/A#  A            C#m/G#
        Do, do,           do, do.
        C#m/B         C#m/A#    A         E                              G#/B#
          I  be - lieve in you  and me,  I'm coming to find you,
                       C#m7
        If it takes me all night,
                     A*             E
        Wrong un - til you make it right.
                               G#/B#                   C#m7
        And I won't forget you,         at least I'll try,
                     A      A#dim     Bsus4   B7/A B7/D#
        And run, and run      to - night.
```

Chorus 1
```
            E                    G#/B#
        ‖: Ev'rything will be al - right,
                               C#m7
        Ev'rything will be al - right,
                               A*
        Ev'rything will be al - right. :‖
```

Link 1
```
            A#dim
        Al - right.
            C#m/B   C#m/A#  A C#m/G#
        ‖: Al - right.                    :‖ Play 3 times
            C#m       F#          B  B/A#    G#m
        Al - right,       la, la, la, la, la,    oh, oh.
```

Bridge

           C♯m   F♯
I wasn't shopping for a doll,

                    D♯7   G♯m
To say the least, I thought I'd   seen them all.

                  C♯m   F♯
But then you took me by sur - prise,

                      B
I'm dreaming 'bout those dreamy eyes.

    B/A♯   G♯m
I never knew, I never knew,

                            C♯m   F♯
So take your suitcase, 'cause I don't mind.

                    D♯7   G♯m
And baby doll, I meant it   every time,

                  C♯m   F♯
You don't need to compro - mise.

                      B
I'm dreaming 'bout those dreamy eyes,

    B/A♯   G♯m
I never knew, I never knew,

        F♯   C♯/E♯
But it's   al - right,

Alright.

Chorus 2

   E   G♯/B♯
‖: Ev'rything will be al - right,

                    C♯m7
Ev'rything will be al - right,

                  A*
Ev'rything will be al - right. :‖ *Play 3 times*

Chorus 3

   E   G♯/B♯
Ev'rything will be al - right,

                    C♯m7
Ev'rything will be al - right,

                  A*
Ev'rything will be al - right, will be alright.

Outro

‖: E | G♯/B♯ | C♯m7 | A*   :‖ *Play 3 times*

| E | E   ‖ *Fade out*

For Reasons Unknown

Words & Music by
Brandon Flowers, Dave Keuning, Mark Stoermer & Ronnie Vannucci

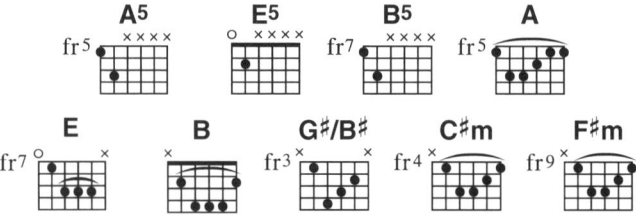

Tune guitar down a semitone

Verse 1

      A5   **E5**
I pack my case, I check my face, I look a little bit older.

              B5
I look a little bit colder.

      A5   **E5**
With one deep breath and one big step, I move a little bit closer.

              B5
I move a little bit closer.

      A5
For reasons unknown.

Verse 2

     A
I caught my stride, I flew and flied.

             E   **B**   **G♯/B♯**
I know if destiny's kind, I've got the rest on my mind.

     C♯m   **A**
But my heart, it don't beat, it don't beat the way it used to,

            E   **B**   **G♯/B♯**
And my eyes, they don't see you no more._____

     C♯m   **A**
And my lips, they don't kiss, they don't kiss the way they used to,

            E   **B**   **G♯/B♯**
And my eyes don't recognise you no more._____

Chorus 1

     E   **F♯m**   **C♯m** **B**
For reasons un - known,

     E   **F♯m**   **C♯m** **B**
For reasons un - known.

Verse 3

              A
There was an open chair,

We sat down in the open chair.
        E   B   G♯/B♯
I said if destiny's kind, I've got the rest on my mind.
      C♯m   A
But my heart, it don't beat, it don't beat the way it used to,
        E   B   G♯/B♯
And my eyes, they don't see you no more. _____
      C♯m   A
And my lips, they don't kiss, they don't kiss the way they used to,
        E   B   G♯/B♯
And my eyes don't recognise you at all. _____

Chorus 2

      E   F♯m C♯m B
For reasons un - known,
      E   F♯m C♯m B
For reasons un - known.

Bridge

      E   F♯m   C♯m   B
I said my heart, it don't beat, it don't beat the way it used to,
      E   F♯m   C♯m   B
And my eyes don't recog - nise you no more.
G♯/B♯ C♯m   A   E   B
And my lips, they don't kiss, they don't kiss the way they used to,
G♯/B♯ C♯m   A   E   B G♯/B♯
And my eyes don't recog - nise you no more.

Chorus 3

𝄆   E   F♯m C♯m B
For reasons un - known.   𝄇 *Play 4 times*

| E | |

Forget About What I Said

Words & Music by
Brandon Flowers, Dave Keuning, Mark Stoermer & Ronnie Vannucci

Tune guitar down a semitone

Intro | Bm | Bm ||

‖: Bm | D | G | A   :‖

Verse 1

(A)   Bm   D
We used to tear it down,
G   A
  But now we just ex - ist.
          Bm   D
The things that I did wrong,
G   A
  I'll bet you've got a list.
      Bm   D
Now I know how you re - member,
        G   A
And those moments that you choose,
      Bm   D
Will de - fine me as a traitor,
        G   A
Stealing everything you lose.

Chorus 1

D   Em
  Forget about what I said,
G
  The lights are gone and the party's over.
Bm   A   Em F♯m
  Forget about what I said.
D   Em
  Forget about what I said,
G
  I'm older now and I know you hear me.
Bm   A   Em F♯m
  Forget about what I said.

Verse 2

    (F♯)   **Bm**   **D**
You'll stay up late tonight,
G   **A**
    You'll turn off your 'phone.
            Bm   **D**
Well you were selfish too,
          G   **A**
But you were never all a - lone.
         Bm   **D**
In those ugly pink a - partments,
          G   **A**
With the hustlers and the kids,
         Bm   **D**
Mapping out some retri - bution.
        G   **A**
Do we have to go through this?

Chorus 2   As Chorus 1

Bridge

G   **Em**   **D**
   All of the stars are   wandering round to - night,
                 G
We used to try them on.
                 Em
And sometimes I hear you,
              A
The galaxy sings your song.
             (D)
And tonight I sing a - long.

Chorus 3

D   **Em**
   Forget about what I said,
G
   The lights are gone and the party's over.
Bm   **A**   **Em** **F♯m**
   Forget about what I said.
D   **Em**
   Forget about what I said,
G
   I'm older now and I know you hear me.
Bm   **A**   **Em** **F♯m**
   Forget about what I said.
Bm   **A**   **Em** **F♯m** **(D)**
   Forget about what I said.

Get Trashed

Words & Music by
Brandon Flowers, Dave Keuning, Mark Stoermer & Ronnie Vannucci

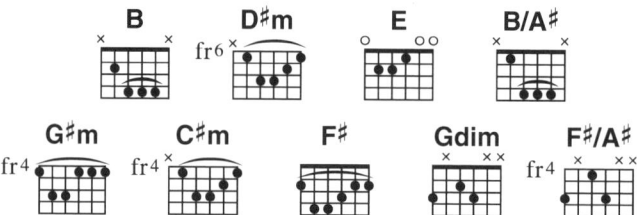

Verse 1

```
        B                D♯m E                B    B/A♯
Sitting here on the bed,  trying to clear my head,
     G♯m                   C♯m      E              F♯
But Brooke you just won't budge, so I look back in - stead.
        B                D♯m E            B   B/A♯
Why'd you go a - way? Useless when I say, hey,
    G♯m          C♯m          E           F♯
Baby I'll be the best, 'cause I'm a jealous mess.
        B                  D♯m
So wash your hands from all this dirt,
        E               B         B/A♯
And take my words for what they're worth.
G♯m            C♯m
Baby I'll be the best,
        E               F♯
But you stand to pro - test,
            B             D♯m
And my stomach has been so abused,
            E           B          B/A♯
Your con - fusion's got me so confused.
        G♯m              C♯m    E              F♯
But ev'rything will be al - right if I get trashed to - night.
```

```
B                   D♯m E              B      B/A♯
Sitting here on the bed,  trying to clear my head,
    G♯m                C♯m      E            F♯
But Brooke you just won't budge, so I look back in - stead.
B                   D♯m E        B     B/A♯
Why'd you go a - way? Useless when I say, hey,
G♯m         C♯m       E          F♯
Baby I'll be the best, 'cause I'm a jealous mess.
          B              D♯m
And my stomach has been so abused,
         E           B          B/A♯
Your con - fusion's got me so confused.
    G♯m                 C♯m   E           F♯   Gdim G♯m F♯/A♯
But ev'rything will be al - right if I get trashed to - night.
```

Instrumental

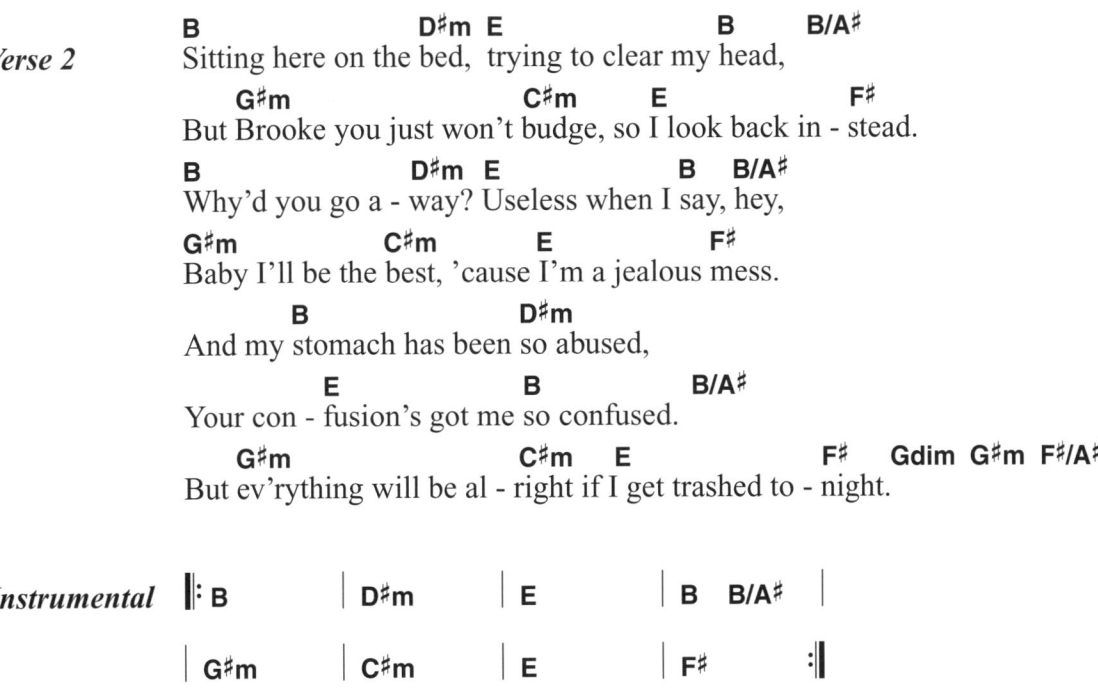

```
‖: B         | D♯m      | E        | B   B/A♯  |

 | G♯m       | C♯m      | E        | F♯       :‖

 | Gdim      | G♯m F♯/A♯| B        ‖
```

Four Winds

Words & Music by
Conor Oberst

Gm   E♭   B♭   Cm   F   F/A   Dm⁷

Intro

| Gm | E♭ | B♭ | Cm | |

| B♭ | Cm | E♭ | E♭ | ||

Verse 1

          Gm   E♭
Your class, your caste, your country, sect, your name or your tribe,

          B♭   Cm
There's people always dying trying to keep them alive.

          B♭   Cm
There's bodies decomposing in con - tainers tonight,

          E♭
In an a - bandoned building where,

Gm   E♭
Squatters made a mural of a Mexican girl,

          B♭   Cm
With fifteen cans of spray paint in a chemical swirl,

                      Cm
She's standing in the ashes at the end of the world,

             Gm
Four winds   blowing through her hair.

Chorus 1

(Gm)   Cm   F   Cm F
But when great Satan's gone, the whore of Ba - by - lon,

          E♭   B♭   E♭   B♭
She just can't su - stain the pressure where it's placed,

          Cm   F
She caves, she caves.

Link 1

| Gm | E♭ | B♭ | Cm | |

| B♭ | Cm | E♭ | E♭ | ‖

Verse 2

      Gm   E♭
The Bible's blind, the Torah's deaf, the Koran is mute,

       B♭   Cm
If you burned them all together you'd get close to the truth still,

       B♭   Cm
They're poring over Sanskrit under Ivy League moons,

            E♭
While shadows lengthen in the sun.

          Gm   E♭
Cast all the school of meditation built to soften the times,

    B♭   Cm
And hold us at the centre while the spiral unwinds.

     B♭   Cm
It's knocking over fences, crossing property lines,

        Gm
Four winds cry until it comes.

Chorus 2

    (Gm)   Cm   F
And it's the sum of man,

                  Cm   F
Slouching towards Bethle - hem.

            E♭   B♭   E♭   B♭
A heart just can't con - tain all of that empty space,

    Cm   F
It breaks, it breaks, it breaks!

Link 2

    Gm E♭   B♭   Cm
      Ooh, ooh.

          B♭
Ooh, ooh.

          Cm
Ooh, ooh.

 E♭
    Ooh, ooh.

Verse 3

(E♭)   **Gm**   **E♭**
Well, I went back by rented Cadillac and company jet,

     B♭   **Cm**
Like a newly orphaned refugee, re - tracing my steps.

       B♭   **Cm**
All the way to Cassadaga to com - mune with the dead,

                       E♭
They said, "You'd   better look alive."

             Gm   **E♭**
And I was off to old Dakota where a geno - cide sleeps,

     B♭   **Cm**
In the black hills, the bad lands, the calloused east.

  B♭   **Cm**
I buried my ballast, I made my peace,

                 E♭
With four winds levelling the pines.

Chorus 3

(Gm)   **Cm**   **F**   **Cm** **F**
But when great Satan's gone, the whore of Ba - by - lon,

      E♭   **B♭**   **E♭**   **B♭**
She just can't re - main with all that outer space,

   F/A   **Gm**
She breaks, she breaks,

   Cm **B♭**   **E♭** **Dm7** **Cm**   **F**
She caves,   she caves,   she breaks.

You'd better look alive.

Outro

‖: **Gm** | **E♭** | **B♭** | **Cm** |

| **B♭** | **Cm** | **E♭** | **E♭** :‖   *Repeat to fade*

Glamorous Indie Rock And Roll

Words & Music by
Brandon Flowers, Dave Keuning, Mark Stoermer & Ronnie Vannucci

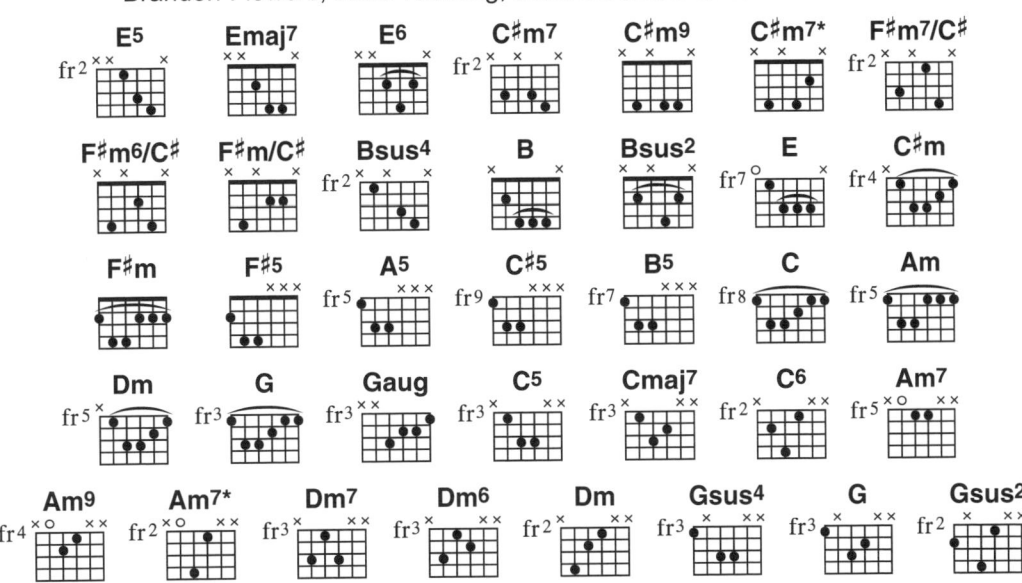

Tune guitar down a semitone

Intro | E5   ‖

Verse 1
    E5   Emaj7 E6   Emaj7 C#m7   C#m9 C#m7*
    Glamor - ous   indie rock 'n' roll is   what I want,

                 C#m9   F#m7/C#   F#m6/C#
It's in my soul, it's what I need._____

F#m/C#   F#m6/C# Bsus4   B Bsus2 B
Indie rock 'n' roll, it's time.

Verse 2
    E5   Emaj7 E6   Emaj7   C#m7   C#m9 C#m7*
    Two of us   flipping through a thrift store magazine,

                 C#m9   F#m7/C# F#m6/C#
She plays the drums, I'm on tambou - rine.

F#m/C#   F#m6/C#   Bsus4   B
Bet your, your bottom dollar on me.

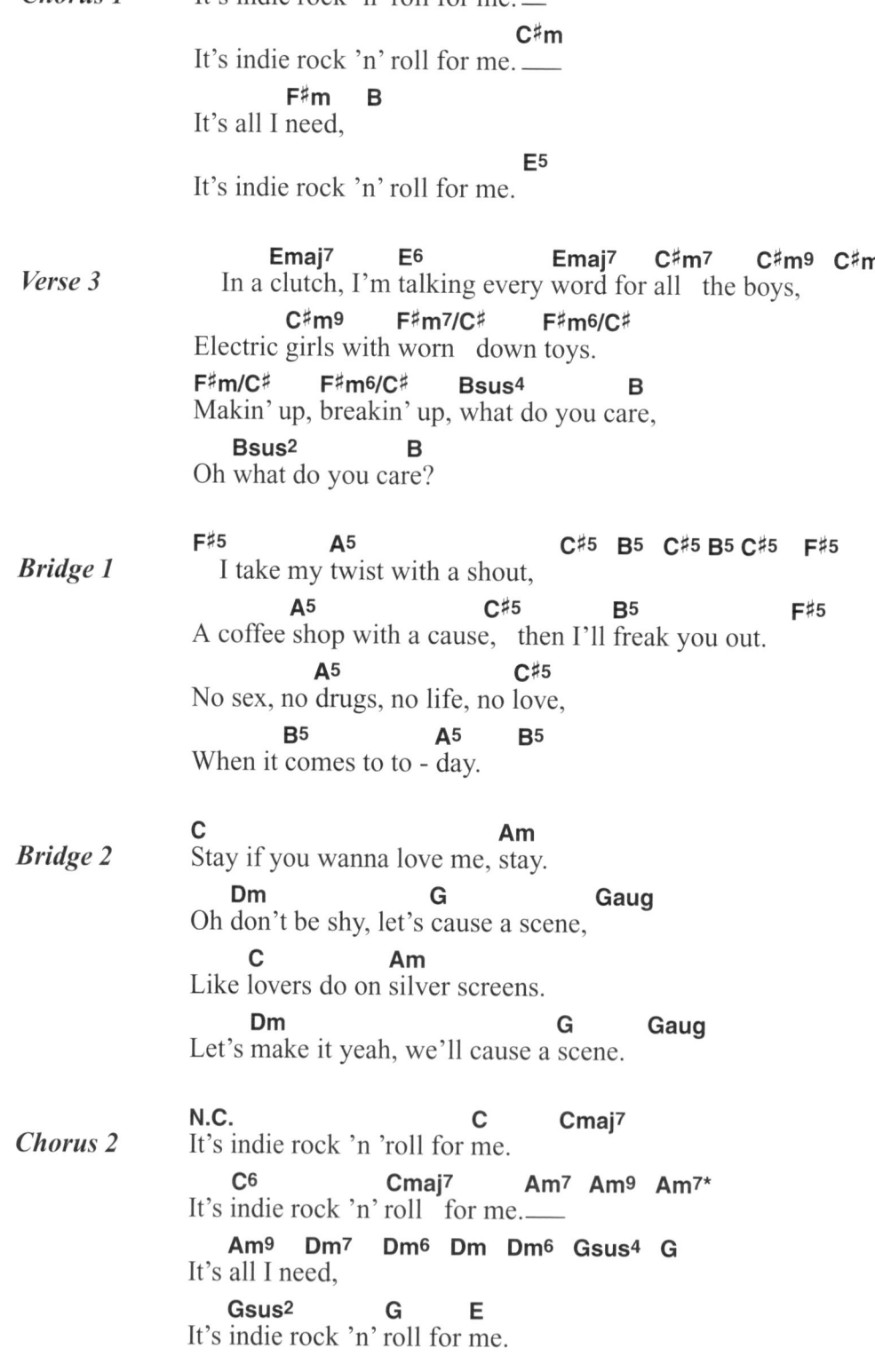

Chorus 1

   Bsus²   **B**   **E**
It's indie rock 'n' roll for me. —

                           C♯m
It's indie rock 'n' roll for me. ___

       F♯m   **B**
It's all I need,

                        E⁵
It's indie rock 'n' roll for me.

Verse 3

       Emaj⁷   **E⁶**   **Emaj⁷** **C♯m⁷**   **C♯m⁹** **C♯m⁷***
In a clutch, I'm talking every word for all   the boys,

         C♯m⁹   **F♯m⁷/C♯**   **F♯m⁶/C♯**
Electric girls with worn   down toys.

F♯m/C♯   **F♯m⁶/C♯**   **Bsus⁴**   **B**
Makin' up, breakin' up, what do you care,

    Bsus²   **B**
Oh what do you care?

Bridge 1

F♯⁵   **A⁵**   **C♯⁵** **B⁵** **C♯⁵ B⁵ C♯⁵** **F♯⁵**
   I take my twist with a shout,

      A⁵   **C♯⁵**   **B⁵**   **F♯⁵**
A coffee shop with a cause,   then I'll freak you out.

        A⁵   **C♯⁵**
No sex, no drugs, no life, no love,

     B⁵   **A⁵**   **B⁵**
When it comes to to - day.

Bridge 2

  C   **Am**
Stay if you wanna love me, stay.

    Dm   **G**   **Gaug**
Oh don't be shy, let's cause a scene,

     C   **Am**
Like lovers do on silver screens.

    Dm   **G**   **Gaug**
Let's make it yeah, we'll cause a scene.

Chorus 2

N.C.   **C**   **Cmaj⁷**
It's indie rock 'n 'roll for me.

    C⁶   **Cmaj⁷**   **Am⁷ Am⁹ Am⁷***
It's indie rock 'n' roll for me.___

   Am⁹   **Dm⁷** **Dm⁶ Dm Dm⁶ Gsus⁴ G**
It's all I need,

   Gsus²   **G**   **E**
It's indie rock 'n' roll for me.

Chorus 3

                                                         C#m
In a clutch, I'm talking every word for all the boys,

               F#m
It's all I need. ——

                     B
Makin' up, breakin' up, what do you care,

                            E
It's indie rock 'n' roll for me. —

Chorus 4

                                                   C#m
Two of us, flipping through a thrift store magazine,

               F#m
It's all I need. ——

                     B
Makin' up, breakin' up, what do you care?

                            E5 Emaj7 E6 Emaj7 E5
It's indie rock 'n' roll for me. ——————

Goodnight, Travel Well

Words by Brandon Flowers
Music by Brandon Flowers, Dave Keuning, Mark Stoermer & Ronnie Vannucci

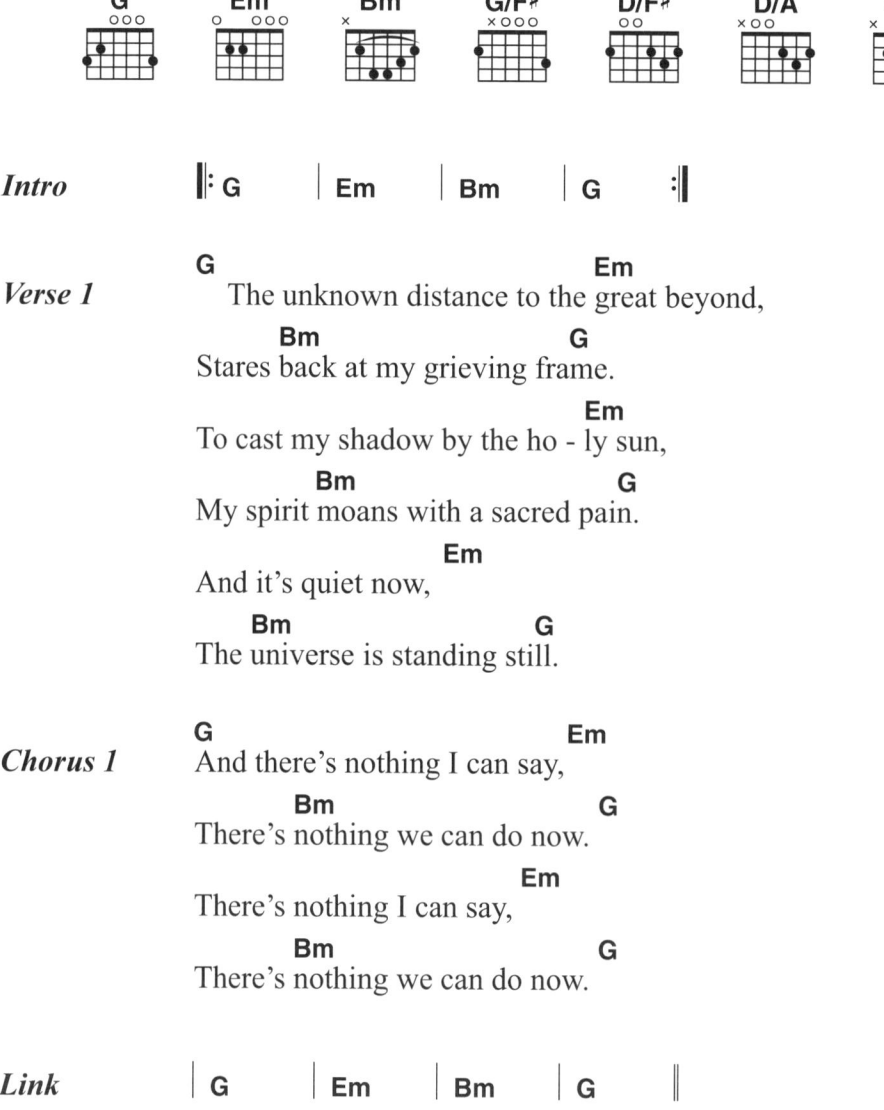

Intro

‖: G | Em | Bm | G :‖

Verse 1

G   Em
The unknown distance to the great beyond,
Bm   G
Stares back at my grieving frame.
                                                    Em
To cast my shadow by the ho - ly sun,
            Bm   G
My spirit moans with a sacred pain.
                                      Em
And it's quiet now,
            Bm   G
The universe is standing still.

Chorus 1

G   Em
And there's nothing I can say,
            Bm   G
There's nothing we can do now.
                                          Em
There's nothing I can say,
            Bm   G
There's nothing we can do now.

Link

| G | Em | Bm | G ‖

Verse 2

    G   Em

And all that stands between the souls release,

       Bm   G

This temporary flesh and bone.

                               Em

We know that it's over now,

       Bm   G

I feel my faded mind begin to roam.

Bridge 1

    G

Every time you fall,

                Em

And every time you try,

       Bm

Every foolish dream,

             G

And every compro - mise.

Every word you spoke,

               Em

And everything you said,

         Bm   G

Everything you left me, rambles in my head.

Chorus 2

    G   Em

And there's nothing I can say,

       Bm   G

There's nothing I can do now.

                          Em

There's nothing I can say,

       Bm   G

There's nothing I can do now.

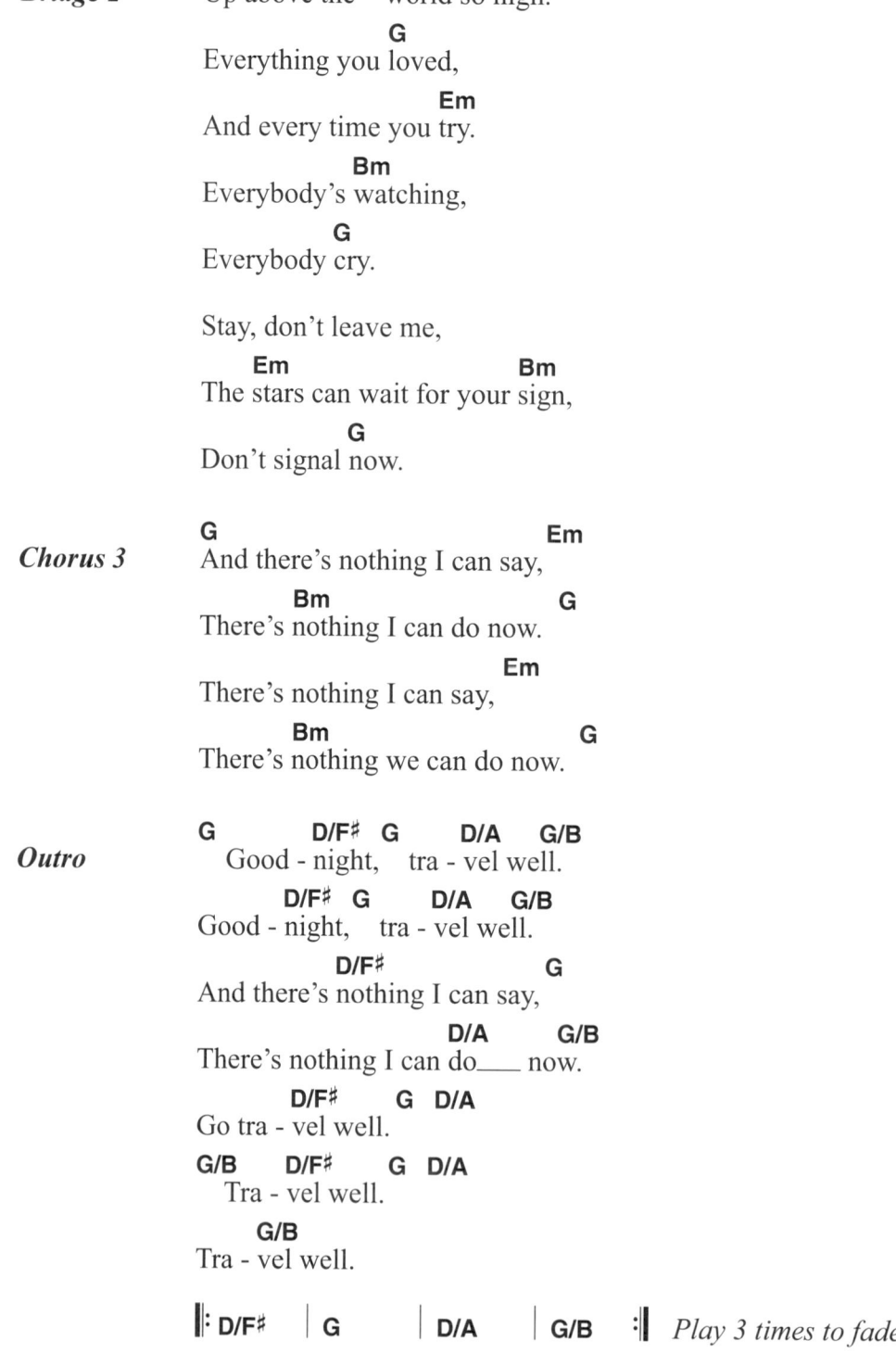

Bridge 2

```
G        G/F♯ Em      G/F♯   Bm  Em  G/F♯
Up above the   world so high.

                     G
Everything you loved,

                        Em
And every time you try.

               Bm
Everybody's watching,

               G
Everybody cry.


Stay, don't leave me,
        Em              Bm
The stars can wait for your sign,
                 G
Don't signal now.
```

Chorus 3

```
G                            Em
And there's nothing I can say,
        Bm                G
There's nothing I can do now.
                            Em
There's nothing I can say,
        Bm                    G
There's nothing we can do now.
```

Outro

```
G        D/F♯ G      D/A   G/B
Good - night,   tra - vel well.

         D/F♯ G      D/A   G/B
Good - night,   tra - vel well.

             D/F♯            G
And there's nothing I can say,
                       D/A    G/B
There's nothing I can do___ now.
         D/F♯      G  D/A
Go tra - vel well.
G/B      D/F♯    G  D/A
  Tra - vel well.
         G/B
Tra - vel well.
```

‖: D/F♯ | G | D/A | G/B :‖ *Play 3 times to fade*

A Great Big Sled

Words & Music by
Brandon Flowers, Dave Keuning, Mark Stoermer & Ronnie Vannucci

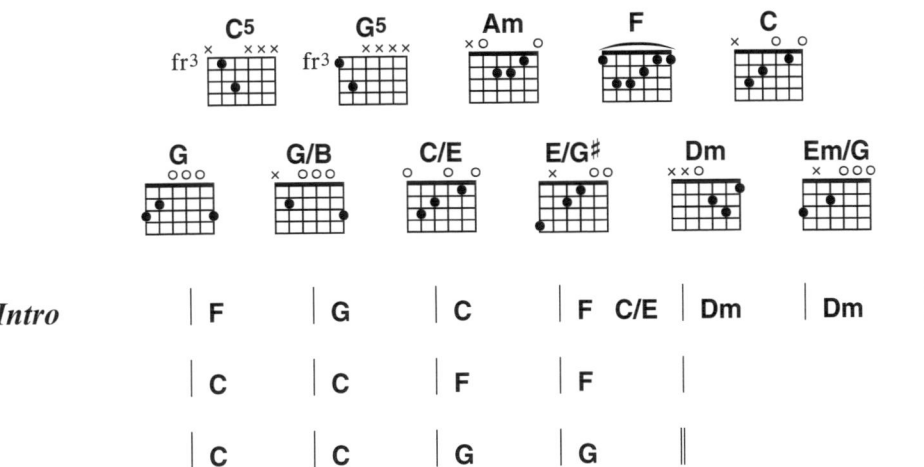

Intro

| F | G | C | F C/E | Dm | Dm | |

| C | C | F | F | |

| C | C | G | G | ‖

Verse 1

N.C. (C)   N.C. (F)
The snowman is shaping up to be an eight but not out of ten.

   C5
The robots awake to find that they've been taped down,

G5   Am
Wondering when they break through these chains.

    F   C
But   little boys have action toys for brains,

                  G
I'm living proof it can last a long time.

Verse 2

           C
Now the girls up the street are innocent and sweet,

          F
While they're all in bed.

         C
They got their makeup and dreams of wonderland,

         G
Sprinkled in - side their heads.

Am
Soon they will change,

        F   C
But tonight   Hollywood Hills never seemed so strange.

                 G   G/B
Their mothers pray it will last a long time.

Chorus 1

             C   **F**   **C/E**   **G**
I wanna roll a - round like a kid in the snow,

  E/G♯   **Am**   **F**   **C/E** **G**
I wanna re-learn what I already know.

          F   **G**
Just let me take flight dressed in red,

        C   **F**   **C/E Dm**
Through the night on a great big sled.

                  C
I wanna wish you merry Christmas,

Ho, ho, ho.

Verse 3

         C
Now the boys are all grown up,

                F
And they're working their fingers to the bone.

        C
They go a - round chasing them girls on the weekend,

        G
You know they still can't be alone.

      Am
I've been racking my brain,

                  F
With thoughts of peace and love.

                C
How on earth did we get so mixed up?

          G
I pray to God it don't last a long time.

Chorus 2

             C   **F**   **C/E**   **G**
I wanna roll a - round like a kid in the snow,

  E/G♯   **Am**   **F**   **C/E** **G**
I wanna re - learn what I already know.

          F   **G**
Just let me take flight dressed in red,

        C   **F**   **C/E Am**
Through the night on a great big sled.

Bridge

                 Dm
I hear the sound of bells,

                    G
There's something on the roof,

         Em/G   **E/G♯**   **Am G/B G**
I wonder what this night will bring.

Chorus 3
                   C   F   C/E   G
I wanna roll a - round like a kid in the snow,

  E/G♯   Am   F   C/E   G
I wanna re-learn what I already know.

                    F   G
Just let me take flight dressed in red,

           C   F   C/E Dm   G
Through the night on a great big sled.

Outro
                           C
I wanna wish you merry Christmas.

          G   F
Can't do that.

                           C
I wanna wish you merry Christmas.

          G   F C/E Dm C
Can't do that.

Human

Words by Brandon Flowers
Music by Brandon Flowers, Dave Keuning, Mark Stoermer & Ronnie Vannucci

Bb   Dm   Eb   F   Gm   Cm   F#dim7

Intro
| Bb | Bb | Bb | Bb ‖

Verse 1

Bb   Dm   Eb   Bb
I did my best to notice when the call came down the line,

      F   Gm   Bb   F
Up to the platform of sur - render, I was brought but I was kind.

Bb   Dm   Eb   Gm
And sometimes I get nervous when I see an open door,

     Eb   F   Bb
Close your eyes, clear your heart,   cut the cord.

Chorus 1

Bb   Dm   Eb   Bb
  Are we human   or are we dancer?

F   Gm   Eb   F
  My sign is vital,   my hands are cold.

      Bb   Dm   Gm
And I'm on my knees looking for the answer,

      Cm   Eb   Bb
Are we human   or are we dancer?

Link 1
| Bb | Dm | Eb | Bb |

| F | Gm | Eb | F ‖

Verse 2

(F)   Bb   Dm   Eb   Bb
  Pay my re - spects to grace and virtue, send my con - dolences to good.

           F   Gm
Give my re - gards to soul and romance,

         Eb   F
They always did the best they could.

     Bb   Dm   Eb   Gm
And so long to de - votion, you taught me everything I know,

     Eb   F   Bb
Wave good - bye, wish me well,   you've got to let me go.

Chorus 2

B♭   Dm E♭   B♭
  Are we human   or are we dancer?

F   Gm E♭   F
  My sign is vital,   my hands are cold.

    B♭   Dm   Gm
And I'm on my knees looking for the answer,

     Cm   E♭   B♭
Are we human   or are we dancer?

Bridge

(Dm)   E♭   F   F♯dim7   Gm
 Will your system be al - right when you dream of home to - night?

    E♭
There is no message we're receiving,

F
Let me know, is your heart still beating?

B♭   F   Gm
  Are we human or   are we dancer?

E♭   F Dm   E♭
  My sign is vital,   my hands are cold.

    B♭   Dm   Gm
And I'm on my knees looking for the answer,

You've got to let me know.

Chorus 3

B♭   Dm E♭   B♭
  Are we human   or are we dancer?

F   Gm E♭   F
  My sign is vital,   my hands are cold.

    B♭   Dm   Gm
And I'm on my knees looking for the answer,

     Cm   E♭   (B♭)
Are we human   or are we dancer?

Link 2

B♭	Dm	E♭	B♭	
F	Gm	E♭	F	
B♭	Dm	E♭	Gm	

Outro

(Gm) E♭   Gm   F
Are we human or are we dancer?

     E♭   Cm   B♭
Are we human   or are we dancer?

I Can't Stay

Words by Brandon Flowers
Music by Brandon Flowers, Dave Keuning, Mark Stoermer & Ronnie Vannucci

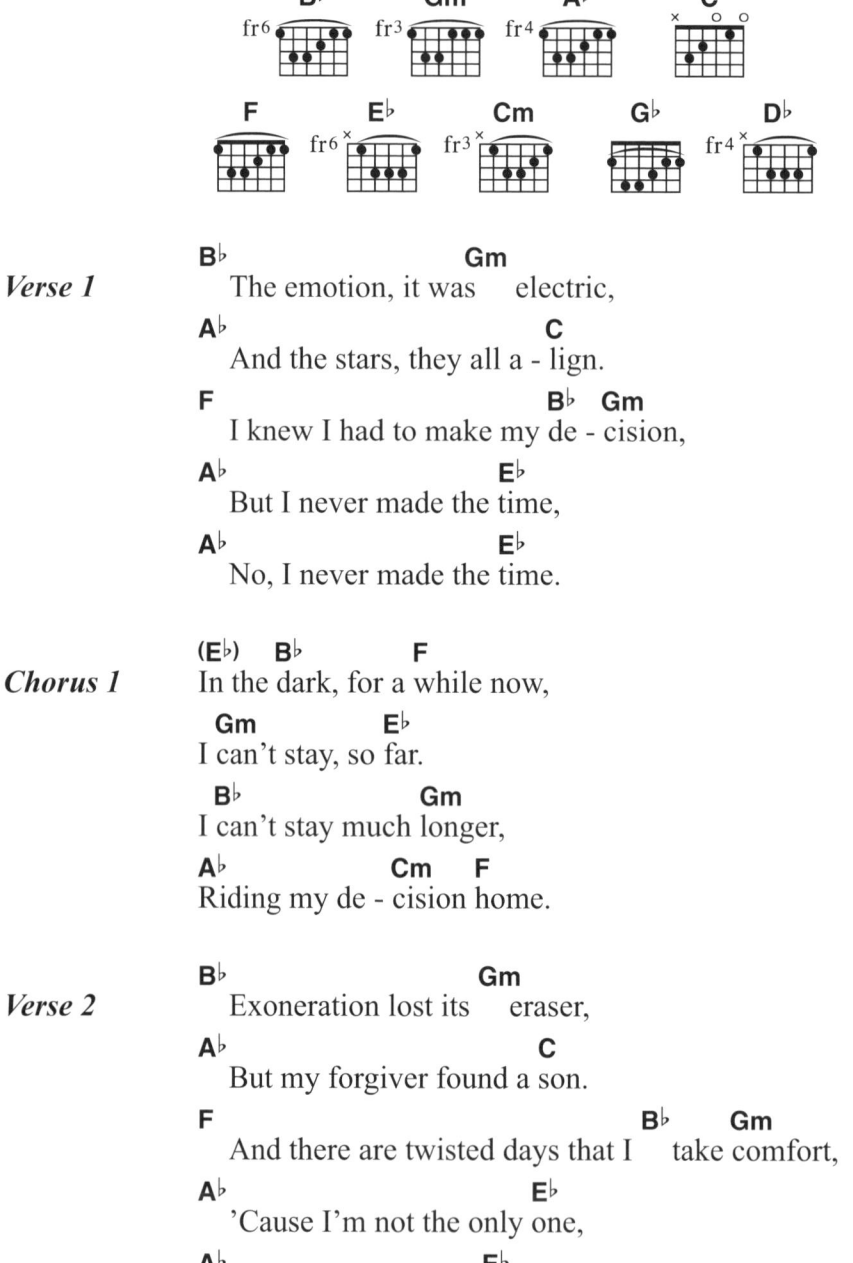

Verse 1

Bb   Gm
   The emotion, it was   electric,
Ab   C
And the stars, they all a - lign.
F   Bb Gm
I knew I had to make my de - cision,
Ab   Eb
But I never made the time,
Ab   Eb
No, I never made the time.

Chorus 1

(Eb) Bb   F
In the dark, for a while now,
Gm   Eb
I can't stay, so far.
Bb   Gm
I can't stay much longer,
Ab   Cm   F
Riding my de - cision home.

Verse 2

Bb   Gm
   Exoneration lost its   eraser,
Ab   C
But my forgiver found a son.
F   Bb Gm
   And there are twisted days that I   take comfort,
Ab   Eb
  'Cause I'm not the only one,
Ab   Eb
No, I'm not the only one.

Chorus 2

  (E♭) B♭   **F**
In the dark, for a while now,

    Gm   **E♭**
I can't stay very far.

   B♭   **Gm**
I can't stay much longer,

  A♭   **Cm** **F**
  Riding my de - cision home.

Link | **B♭** | **B♭**   ‖

Bridge

  G♭   **D♭**   **A♭**
  Now, there's a majesty   at my doorstep,

  G♭   **D♭**   **A♭**
  And there's a little boy   in her arms.

  G♭   **D♭** **B♭**
  Now, we'll parade around without game plans,

  G♭   **F**
  Obligation or a - larm.

Chorus 3

  (F) B♭   **F**
In the dark, for a while now,

    Gm   **E♭**
I can't stay very far.

   B♭   **Gm**
I can't stay much longer,

  A♭   **Cm** **F**
  Riding my de - cision home.

Chorus 4

  (F) B♭   **F**
In the dark, for a while now,

    Gm   **E♭**
I can't stay so far.

   B♭   **Gm**
I can't stay much longer,

  A♭   **Cm** **F**
  Riding my de - cision home,

        B♭   **F** **Gm** **E♭** **B♭** **Gm** **A♭**
In the dark.   *Fade out*

Jenny Was A Friend Of Mine

Words & Music by
Brandon Flowers, Dave Keuning, Mark Stoermer & Ronnie Vannucci

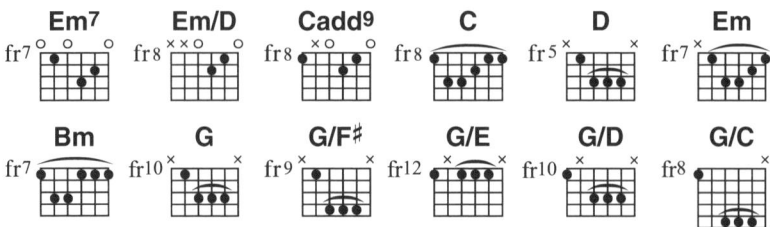

Tune guitar down a semitone

Intro | Em⁷ | Em⁷ | Em⁷ | Em⁷ ‖

‖: Em⁷ | Em/D | Cadd⁹ | Cadd⁹ :‖

Verse 1

Em⁷   Em/D   Cadd⁹
We took a walk that night, but it wasn't the same,

Em⁷   Em/D   Cadd⁹
We had a fight on the promenade out in the rain.

Em⁷   Em/D   Cadd⁹
She said she loved me, but she had somewhere to go.

Em⁷   Em/D
She couldn't scream while I held her close,

   Cadd⁹
I swore I'd never let her go.

Chorus 1

   C   D
Tell me what you wanna know,

      Em   Bm
Oh come on, oh come on, oh come on.

         C   D
There ain't no motive for this crime,

G   G/F♯ G/E   G/D
Jenny was a friend of mine.

         G/C   G/D   Em⁷ Em/D Cadd⁹
So come on, oh come on, oh come on. Oh, oh, oh.

Link 1 | Em⁷ | Em/D | Cadd⁹ | Cadd⁹ ‖

Verse 2

Em⁷   Em/D   Cadd⁹
I know my rights, I've been here all day and it's time,

Em⁷   Em/D   Cadd⁹
For me to go, so let me know if it's al - right.

Em⁷   Em/D   Cadd⁹
I just can't take this, I swear I told you the truth.

Em⁷   Em/D
She couldn't scream while I held her close,

Cadd⁹
I swore I'd never let her go.

Chorus 2

C   D
Tell me what you wanna know,

       Em   Bm
Oh come on, oh come on, oh come on.

      C   D
And then you whisper in my ear,

G   G/F♯   G/E   G/D
I know what you're doing here.

       G/C   G/D
So come on, oh come on, oh come on.

      C   D
There ain't no motive for this crime,

G   G/F♯ G/E   G/D
Jenny was a friend of mine.

       G/C   G/D   Em⁷
Oh come on, oh come on, oh come on. Oh, oh, oh.

Link 2

‖: Em⁷ | Em⁷ | Em⁷ | Em⁷   :‖
(Oh)

Outro

‖: Em⁷ | Em/D | Cadd⁹ | Cadd⁹ :‖   *Play 4 times*

| Em⁷   ‖

Joseph, Better You Than Me

Words & Music by
Elton John, Neil Tennant & Brandon Flowers

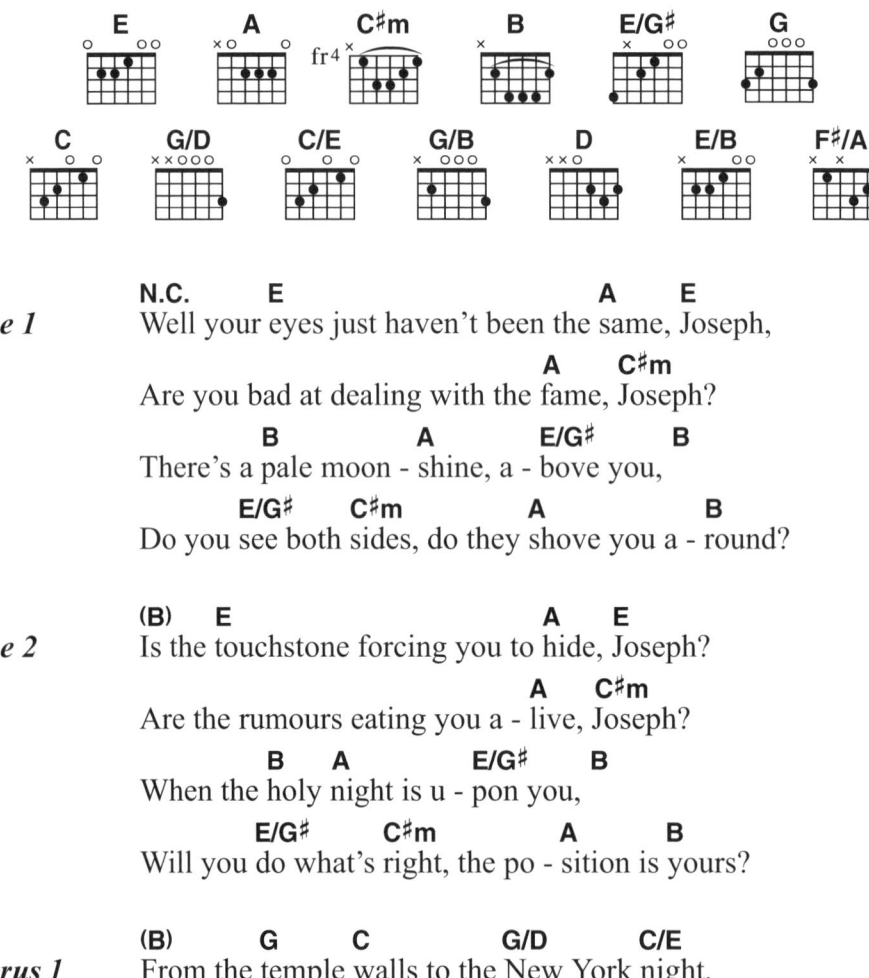

Verse 1

N.C.   E   A   E
Well your eyes just haven't been the same, Joseph,

                              A   C#m
Are you bad at dealing with the fame, Joseph?

        B   A   E/G#   B
There's a pale moon - shine, a - bove you,

       E/G#   C#m   A   B
Do you see both sides, do they shove you a - round?

Verse 2

(B)   E   A   E
Is the touchstone forcing you to hide, Joseph?

                           A   C#m
Are the rumours eating you a - live, Joseph?

        B A   E/G#   B
When the holy night is u - pon you,

       E/G#   C#m   A   B
Will you do what's right, the po - sition is yours?

Chorus 1

(B)   G   C   G/D   C/E
From the temple walls to the New York night,

       G/B   D   C
Our decisions rest on a child.

         G   C
When she took her stand,

       G/B   C/E
Did she hold your hand?

       G/B   D   C
Will your faith stand still or run a - way,

       G
Run a - way?

Guitar solo

| E | B | E | E | |
| E | B | C♯m | C♯m ‖

Verse 3

(C♯m)   E   A
When they've driven you so far,
           E/B
That you think you're gonna drop,
      E   A   C♯m
Do you wish you were back there at the   carpenter shop?
        B   A
With the plane and the lathe,
         E/G♯   B
The work never drove you mad.
         E/G♯   C♯m
You're a maker, a crea - tor,
     A   B
Not just   somebody's dad.

Chorus 2

(B)   G   C   G/D   C/E
From the temple walls to the New York night,
        G/B   D   C
Our de - cisions rest on a man.
       G   C
When I take the stand,
      G/D   C/E
Will he hold my hand?
      G/B   D   C
Will my faith stand still or run a - way,
       E
Run a - way?

Bridge

E   A
And the desert,
    B   E   C♯m
It's a hell of a place to find heaven.
A   B   C♯m
Forty years lost in the wilderness looking for God.
      A   B
And you climb to the top of the mountain,
          B   E
Looking down on the city
     F♯/A♯   A
Where you were born.
                     B
Oh the years since you left gave you time to sit back and reflect.

Outro

```
     E       A          E/G♯        B
      Better you than me, (Better you than me.)
     E       A          E/G♯  B
       Better you than me, yeah.
             E     A          E/G♯            B           (E)
      Well the Holy night is u - pon you, (better you, better you)
             E       A              E/G♯            B        E
      Do you see both sides, do they shove you a - round?____
          A               E/G♯    B
      Better you than me, Joseph,
          E                        A
      Better you than me, (better you than me,)
     E/G♯            E       A
     Joseph, Joseph, Joseph, Joseph,
             E/G♯
      Than me.
          B
      Better you than me.
     E        A
       Better you than me.
          E/G♯        B
      Better you, better you than me.
               E
      Well your eyes just haven't been the same, Joseph.
```

Joy Ride

Words by Brandon Flowers
Music by Brandon Flowers, Dave Keuning, Mark Stoermer & Ronnie Vannucci

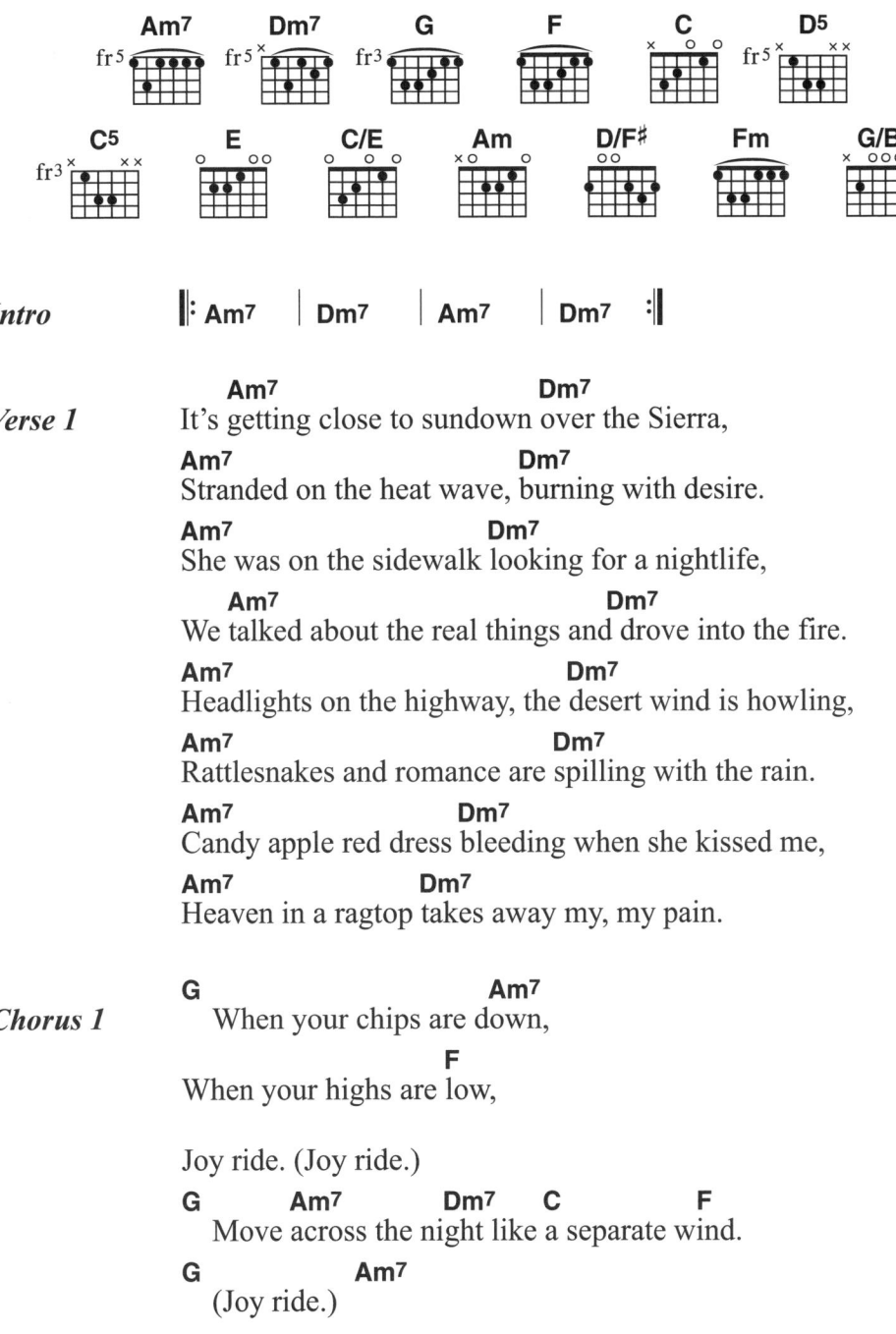

Intro ‖: Am7 | Dm7 | Am7 | Dm7 :‖

Verse 1

        Am7   Dm7
It's getting close to sundown over the Sierra,

Am7   Dm7
Stranded on the heat wave, burning with desire.

Am7   Dm7
She was on the sidewalk looking for a nightlife,

      Am7   Dm7
We talked about the real things and drove into the fire.

Am7   Dm7
Headlights on the highway, the desert wind is howling,

Am7   Dm7
Rattlesnakes and romance are spilling with the rain.

Am7   Dm7
Candy apple red dress bleeding when she kissed me,

Am7   Dm7
Heaven in a ragtop takes away my, my pain.

Chorus 1

G   Am7
   When your chips are down,

                   F
When your highs are low,

Joy ride. (Joy ride.)

G   Am7   Dm7   C   F
   Move across the night like a separate wind.

G   Am7
   (Joy ride.)

Link 1   ‖: Am7 | Dm7 | Am7 | Dm7 :‖

Verse 2

Am7   Dm7
Pulled up to a motel, vacancy was buzzing,
Am7   Dm7
Pink and dirty neon settled on the hood.
Am7   D5   C5
Wrapped her arms around me, come a lit - tle closer,
Am7
Stumbled in the twilight and fell onto the floor.
                    D5   C5
Lovin' Mona Lisa, dreaming of the free world,
Am7   D5   C5
Lipstick on the nightstand and demons at the door.

Chorus 2

G   Am7
   When your chips are down,
                              F
When your highs are low,

Joy ride. (Joy ride.)
G   Am7   Dm7   C   F
   Move across the night like a separate wind.
G
(Joy ride.)

Chorus 3

G   Am7
   When your hopes and dreams
                    F
Lose the will to go,

Joy ride. (Joy ride.)
G   Am7   Dm7
   Reaching for the light,
              C   F   E
More than we can win. (Joy ride.)

Bridge

C/E   G   Am
And something in the distance,

F
A glorious existence.

C/E G   Am
A simple celebration,

D/F♯
A place you've never been before.

Dm7
Why don't you kiss me,

And tell me that you want it?

Fm
Why don't you kiss me?

Interlude

G   Am7
Oh, oh, oh, oh, oh, oh, oh, oh, oh.

F
Oh, oh, oh, oh, oh, oh, oh, oh, oh, oh.

Chorus 4

G   Am7
Reach - ing for the light,

Dm7   F   G
More than we can win.

Dm7   G
When your chips are down,

Dm7
(When your chips are down,)

Fm
When your highs are low,

C   Am   F E
Joy ride. (Joy ride.)

Am7   F
All your hopes and dreams,

Dm7   G/B
All you need to know,

C   Am C F Am7
Joy ride. (Joy ride.)

Leave The Bourbon
On The Shelf

Words & Music by
Brandon Flowers, Dave Keuning, Mark Stoermer & Ronnie Vannucci

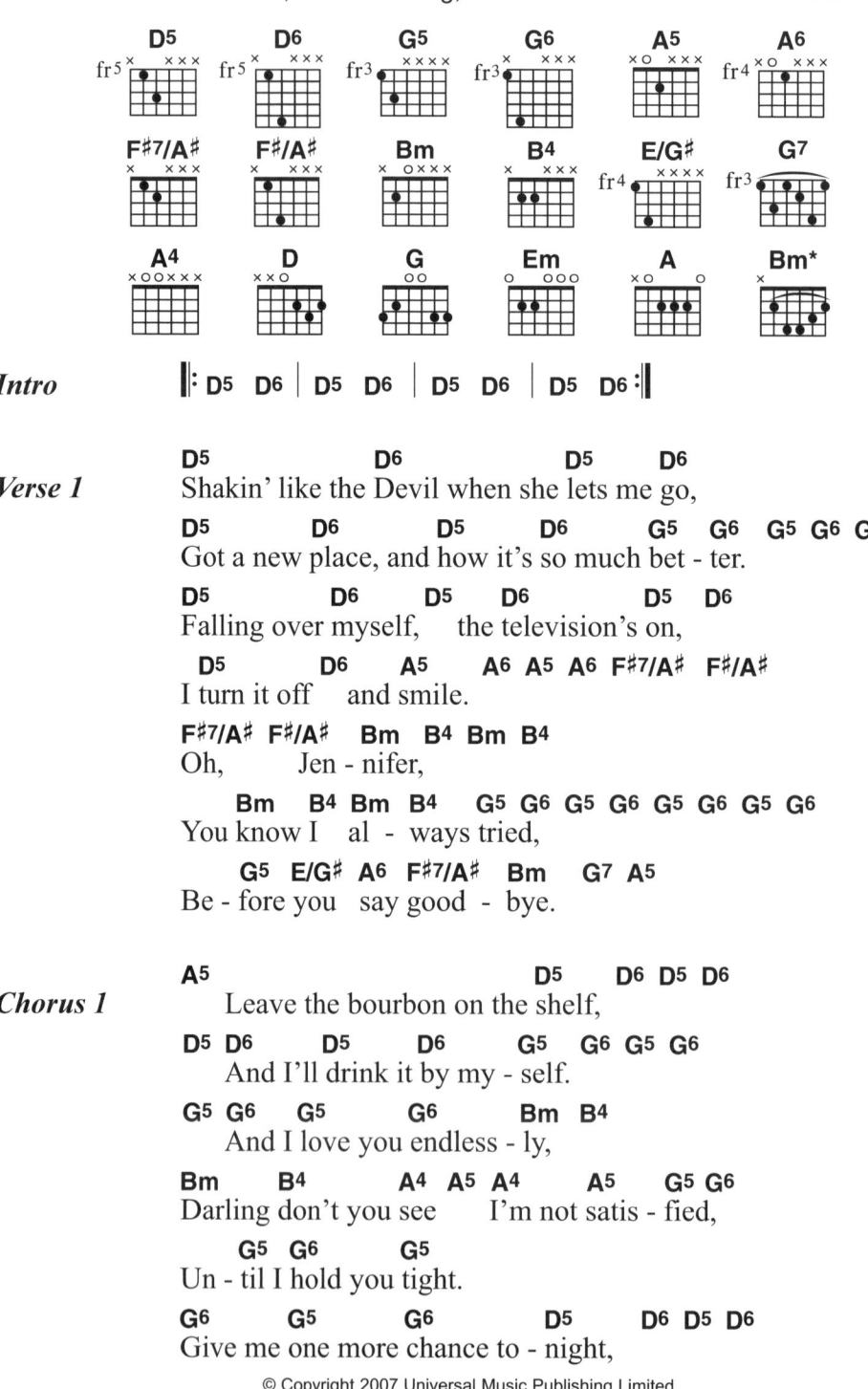

Intro   ‖: D5 D6 | D5 D6 | D5 D6 | D5 D6 :‖

Verse 1

D5   D6   D5   D6
Shakin' like the Devil when she lets me go,

D5   D6   D5   D6   G5 G6 G5 G6 G5 G6 G5 G6
Got a new place, and how it's so much bet - ter.

D5   D6   D5   D6   D5   D6
Falling over myself,   the television's on,

   D5   D6   A5   A6 A5 A6 F#7/A# F#/A#
I turn it off   and smile.

F#7/A# F#/A#   Bm   B4 Bm B4
Oh,   Jen - nifer,

     Bm   B4 Bm B4   G5 G6 G5 G6 G5 G6 G5 G6
You know I   al - ways tried,

     G5 E/G# A6 F#7/A#   Bm   G7 A5
Be - fore you   say good - bye.

Chorus 1

A5   D5   D6 D5 D6
      Leave the bourbon on the shelf,

D5 D6   D5   D6   G5   G6 G5 G6
   And I'll drink it by my - self.

G5 G6   G5   G6   Bm   B4
   And I love you endless - ly,

Bm   B4   A4 A5 A4   A5   G5 G6
Darling don't you see   I'm not satis - fied,

   G5 G6   G5
Un - til I hold you tight.

G6   G5   G6   D5   D6 D5 D6
Give me one more chance to - night,

D5 D6   D5   D6   G5   G6 G5 G6
      And I swear I'll make it right.

G5 G6   G5   G6   Bm   B4
     But you ain't got time for this,

        Bm   B4   A4   A5
And that wreckin'   bell is ringin',

      A4   A5   G5   G6 G5 G6 G5 G6
And I'm not satis - fied,

      G5   G6
Un - til I hold you.

Verse 2

D   G
Jennifer, tell me where I stand,

          Em   A   F♯/A♯
And who's that boy holdin' your hand?

      Bm*   G
Oh, Jen - nifer, you know I always tried,

     G5   E/G♯ A6   F♯7/A♯   Bm   G7 A5
Be - fore you   say good - bye.

Chorus 2

A5   D
Leave the bourbon on the shelf,

          G
And I'll drink it by my - self.

         Bm   A
And I never liked your hair or those people that you lie with.

      G
And I'm not satis - fied,

      A
Until I hold you tight.

        Bm
And I love you endless - ly,

      A   G
Darling don't you see I can't be satis - fied,

      D
Until I hold you tight.

Chorus 3

N.C.(D)
Leave the bourbon on the shelf,

And I'll drink it by myself.

And I'll love you endlessly,

Darling don't you see,

I'm not satisfied.

Losing Touch

Words by Brandon Flowers
Music by Brandon Flowers, Dave Keuning, Mark Stoermer & Ronnie Vannucci

E   B   F♯   G♯m   G♯5   C♯5   F♯7   B6

Intro | E | B | F♯ | G♯m |

| E | B | F♯ | F♯ ‖

‖: G♯5 | G♯5 | C♯5 | C♯5 :‖

Verse 1

G♯5
Console me in my darkest hour,
C♯5   G♯5
Convince me that the truth is always grey.

Caress me in your velvet chair,
C♯5   (E)
Conceal me from the ghosts you cast a - way.

Chorus 1

E   B
I ain't in no hurry,
      F♯   G♯m   E
You go run and tell your friends I'm losing touch.
                              B   F♯
Fill their heads with rumours of impending doom,
            (G♯5)
It must be true.

Link 1 | G#5 | G#5 | C#5 | C#5 ‖

Verse 2

G#5
    Console me in my darkest hour,
C#5   G#5
    And tell me that you always hear my cries.

    I wonder what you've got conspired,
C#5
    I'm sure it dons a consolation prize.

Chorus 2

  E   B
    I ain't in no hurry,
      F#   G#m   E
You go run and tell your friends I'm losing touch.
              B   F#
Fill the night with stories, the legend grows,

Bridge 1

(F#)   B   F#
Of how you got lost.
        C#5   G#5   E
But you made your way back home,
        B   F#
You sold your soul,
        C#5 G#5   E   F#
Like a Roman vaga - bond, yeah.

Verse 3

G#5
    I heard you found a wishing well in the city,

    Console me in my darkest hour,
                (E)
Then you throw me down.

Chorus 3

  E   B
  I ain't in no hurry,

      F♯   G♯m   E
You go run and tell your friends I'm losing touch.

                           B   F♯
Fill your crown with ru - mours,

F♯7   E   B F♯
  Impending doom,

              G♯m   E B F♯
It must be true.

Bridge 2

  B F♯   C♯5   G♯5   E
  But you made your way back home,

                 B   F♯   C♯5   G♯5   E
You sold your soul   like a Roman vagabond.

                   B   F♯
And about how you got lost,

          C♯5   G♯5   E
But you made your way back home.

                   B   F♯
You went and sold your soul,

        C♯5   G♯5   E
An al - legiance dead and gone.

I'm losing touch.

Outro   ‖: B F♯ | C♯5 G♯5 | E | E |

                | B F♯ | C♯5 G♯5 | E | E   :‖ B6   ‖

Midnight Show

Words & Music by
Brandon Flowers, Dave Keuning, Mark Stoermer & Ronnie Vannucci

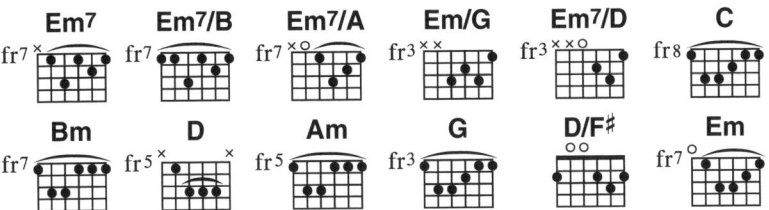

Tune guitar down a semitone

Intro | Em7 | Em7 | Em7/B | Em7/B |

| Em7/A | Em7/A | Em/G | Em7/D ‖

Verse 1
Em7
I know what you want,

Em7/B
I wanna take you a midnight show tonight,

Em7
If you can keep a secret.

Em7/B
I got a blanket in the back seat on my mind,

C　　　　　　**Bm**　　　　**Em7**
And a little place that sits beneath the sky.

Chorus 1
　　　　　　　C　　　　**Bm**
She turned her face to speak,

　　　　　　D
But no-one heard her cry.

N.C.　　　　**Em7**　　**Em7/B**
Drive faster, boy._____

　　　　　　　　Em7/A Em/G　　　**Em7/D**
Drive faster, boy._____ Ye - ah.

Verse 2

Em⁷
I know there's a hope,

There's too many people trying to help me cope.

Em⁷/B
You got a real short skirt,

Em⁷
I wanna look up, look up, look up, yeah, yeah.

We were just in time,

Em⁷/B
Let me take a little more off your mind.

Em⁷
There's something in my head,

Somewhere in the back said:

Em⁷/B
We were just a good thing,

We were such a good thing.

Chorus 2

C   Bm   Em⁷
Make it go a - way without a word,

      C   Bm
But promise me you'll stay,

               D   N.C.
And fix these things I've hurt.

                 Em⁷ Em⁷/B
Oh make it go away,   oh.——

          Em⁷/G   Em/G   Em⁷/D
Drive faster,   boy.—— Ye - ah, oh no.

Solo

| Em⁷ | Em⁷ | Em⁷/B | Em⁷/B |

(no.)

| Em⁷/A | Em⁷/A | Em/G | Em⁷/D ‖

Bridge

     C   **Bm**   **Em⁷**

Oh crashing tide can't hide a guilty girl,

          C   **Bm**   **Em⁷**

With jealous hearts that start with gloss and curls.

     C   **Bm**   **Am**

I took my baby's breath beneath the chandelier

                G

Of stars in atmosphere,

            D/F♯   **D**   **Em⁷**   **Em⁷/B**

And watch her disappear   into the midnight   show.＿＿＿

Chorus 3

           Em⁷/A   **Em/G**   **Em⁷/D**

A-faster,   a-faster, a-faster, a-fast - er,   faster,   a-faster.

      Em⁷

Oh no, no, no, no, no, no.

Em⁷/B

No, no, no, no, no.

      Em⁷/A

If you can keep a secret,

       Em/G   **Em⁷/D**   **Em⁷**   **Em⁷/B**   **Em⁷/A**

Well baby I can keep, you can keep a se - cret.

       Em/G   **Em⁷/D**   **Em⁷**   **Em⁷/B**

If you can keep a secret, I can keep a se - cret.

      Em⁷/A

If you can keep a secret,

       Em/G   **Em⁷/D**   **Em⁷**

Well baby I can keep, you can keep a se - cret.

Outro
keyboard

‖: **Em** | **Am** | **C** | **G** **D** :‖

| **Em**   ‖

Mr. Brightside

Words & Music by
Brandon Flowers, Dave Keuning, Mark Stoermer & Ronnie Vannucci

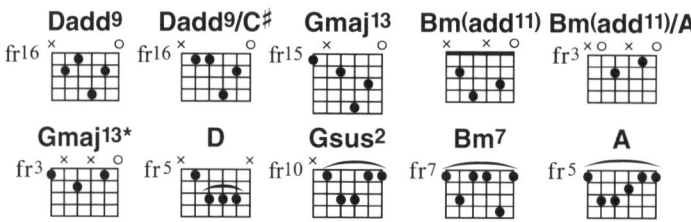

Tune guitar down a semitone

Intro | Dadd⁹ | Dadd⁹/C♯ | Gmaj¹³ | Gmaj¹³ ‖

Verse 1

Dadd⁹   Dadd⁹/C♯   Gmaj¹³
Coming out of my cage and I've been doing just fine,

                                     Dadd⁹
Gotta, gotta be down, because I want it all.

                Dadd⁹/C♯   Gmaj¹³
It started out with a kiss, how did it end up like this?

It was only a kiss, it was only a kiss.

Verse 2

Dadd⁹   Dadd⁹/C♯   Gmaj¹³
Now I'm falling a - sleep and she's calling a cab,

                                  Dadd⁹
While he's having a smoke and she's taking a drag.

                Dadd⁹/C♯   Gmaj¹³
Now they're going to bed and my stomach is sick,

                                  Bm(add¹¹)
And it's all in my head, but she's touching his chest, now.

Bm(add¹¹)/A
He takes off her dress, now.

        Gmaj¹³*
Let me go.

Pre-chorus 1

Bm(add¹¹)   Bm(add¹¹)/A
And I just can't look, it's killing me,

     Gmaj¹³*
And taking control.

Chorus 1

D   Gsus2   Bm7
Jealousy, turning saints in - to the sea,

A   D
Swimming through sick lullabies,

Gsus2   Bm7
Choking on your alibis.

A   D
But it's just the price I pay,

Gsus2   Bm7
Destiny is calling me,

A   D   Gsus2
Open up my eager eyes,_____

Bm7   A
  'Cause I'm Mr. Brightside.

Link 1   ‖: D | Gsus2 | Bm7 | A   :‖

Verse 3   As Verse 1

Verse 4   As Verse 2

Pre-chorus 2   As Pre-chorus 1

Chorus 2   As Chorus 1

Link 2   ‖: D | Gsus2 | Bm7 | A   :‖

Outro   ‖: D | Gsus2 | Bm7 | A   :‖ *Play 4 times*
            I never._____

My List

Words & Music by
Brandon Flowers, Dave Keuning, Mark Stoermer & Ronnie Vannucci

C   C/E   F   G   Am   Em

Intro

| C | C | C | C | C | C |

| C C/E | F C | C C/E | F G |

| Am F | C G | C C/E | F C |

Verse 1

        C   C/E
Let me wrap myself a - round you,
        F   C
Let you show me how I see.
                           C/E
And when you come back in from nowhere,
        F   G   Am
Do you ever think of me?
        F   C   G   C
Your heart   is not able,
         C/E   F   C
Let me show you how much I care.
                        C/E
I need those eyes to tide me over,
           F   C
I'll take your picture when I go.
                     C/E
Gives me strength and gives me patience,
        F   G
But I'll never let you know.
        Am   F
I got nothing on you ba - by,
        C   G   C
But I always said I try.
        C/E   F   C
Let me show you how much I care.

Bridge

Am
Sometimes it gets hard,

And don't she know.

Link 1

‖ C | C | F Em | Am G ‖

Chorus 1

C
Don't give the ghost up, just clench your fist,
                    F   Em   Am   G
You should have known by now you were on my list.
C
Don't give the ghost up, just clench your fist,
                    F   Em   Am   G
You should have known by now you were on my list.
C
Don't give the ghost up, just clench your fist,
                    F   Em   Am   G
You should have known by now you were on my list.

Verse 2

Am   F   C   G   Am
  When your heart   is not able,
        F   C   G   C
And your pray - ers, they're not fables.
        C/E   F
Let me show you, (let me show you.)
        Am   C
Let me show you, (let me show you.)
        C/E   F   C
Let me show you how much I care, oh.

Outro

‖ C C/E | F C | C C/E | F C |

| C | C | C | C | C   ‖

Move Away

Words & Music by
Brandon Flowers, Dave Keuning, Mark Stoermer & Ronnie Vannucci

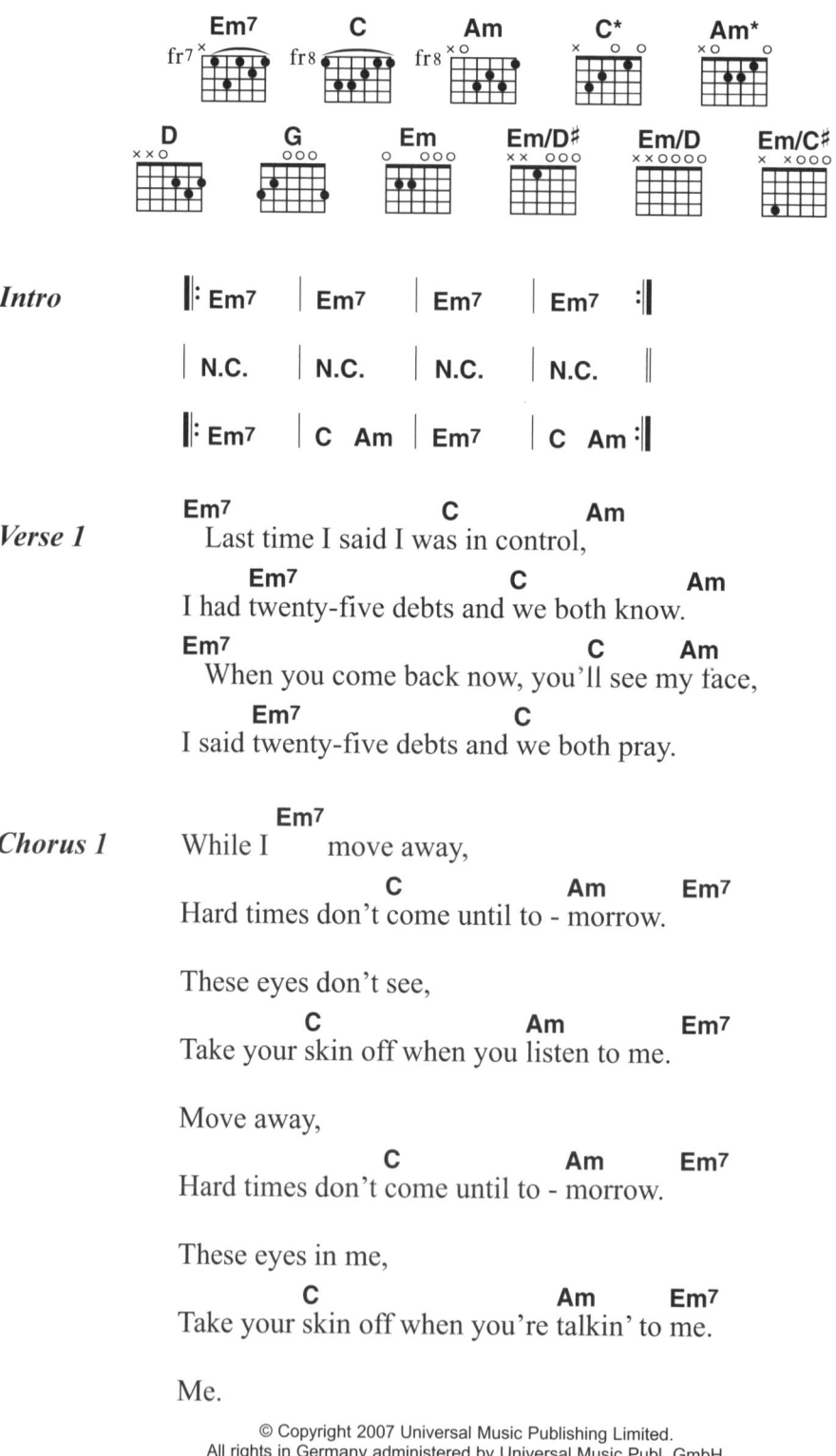

Intro

‖: Em⁷ | Em⁷ | Em⁷ | Em⁷ :‖

| N.C. | N.C. | N.C. | N.C. ‖

‖: Em⁷ | C Am | Em⁷ | C Am :‖

Verse 1

Em⁷   C   Am
Last time I said I was in control,
  Em⁷   C   Am
I had twenty-five debts and we both know.
Em⁷   C Am
 When you come back now, you'll see my face,
  Em⁷   C
I said twenty-five debts and we both pray.

Chorus 1

      Em⁷
While I move away,
       C   Am Em⁷
Hard times don't come until to - morrow.

These eyes don't see,
      C   Am Em⁷
Take your skin off when you listen to me.

Move away,
      C   Am Em⁷
Hard times don't come until to - morrow.

These eyes in me,
     C   Am Em⁷
Take your skin off when you're talkin' to me.

Me.

Verse 2

Em7   C   Am
Oh what a world that we both come in,

     Em7   C   Am
I said hold it to the rock and let it in.

Em7   C   Am
Oh what a world oh that we are in,

     Em7   C
I said hold it to the rock and we're both in.

Chorus 2

          Em7
While I   move away,

                C   Am   Em7
Hard times don't come until to - morrow.

These eyes don't see,

            C   Am   Em7
Tear your skin off when you listen to me.

Move away,

            C   Am   Em7
Hard times don't come until to - morrow.

These eyes don't see,

            C   Am   Em7
Take your skin off when you listen to me.

Bridge

                C*
Don't worry a - bout what might have been,

            Am*   D
Just tell your woman that you're sorry,

          G
And you jumped out of your skin.

          Em
Listen closely to your motto.

               C
Don't worry a - bout what might have been,

        Am   D
Tell the jury that you're sorry,

          Em
And just jump out of your skin.

          Em/D♯
I wanna jump out of my skin,

          Em/D   Em/C♯
I wanna jump out of my skin and watch the clouds

C   Em Em/D♯   Em/D   Em/C♯ C
Move away,   I'm never gonna live it down.

Link

           Em⁷   **C** **Am**
Move a - way.

           Em⁷   **C**   **Am**
Move a - way.   Move,   move,

           Em⁷   **C** **Am**
Move a - way.

           Em⁷   **C** **Am**
Move a - way.

Chorus 3

Em⁷
   Move away,

                      C   **Am**   **Em⁷**
Hard times don't come until to - morrow.

These eyes don't see,
             C   **Am**   **Em⁷**
Take your skin off when you listen to me.

Move away,
                    C   **Am**   **Em⁷**
Hard times don't come until to - morrow.

                        C   **Am**   **Em⁷**
Move away, move away,   move away,   move a - way.——

Outro

‖: **Em⁷** | **C** **Am** | **Em⁷** | **C** **Am** :‖

| **Em**   ‖

90

Neon Tiger

Words by Brandon Flowers
Music by Brandon Flowers, Dave Keuning, Mark Stoermer & Ronnie Vannucci

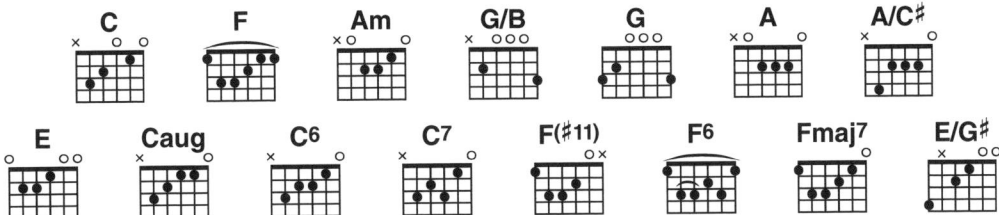

Tune guitar down a semitone

Verse 1

      C
Far from the evergreen of old Assam,

                                 F
Far from the rainfall on the trails of old Sai - gon.

Straight from the poster town of scorn and ritz,

  C
To bring you the wilder side of gold and glitz.

Chorus 1

      C   Am   F   G/B
Run, neon tiger there's a lot on your mind,

G   C   A   A/C#
They promised just to pet you, but don't you let them get you.

     F   E   G
A - way, a - way, oh, run,

              F   G   C
Under the heat of the southwest sun.

Verse 2

    C
You took to the spotlight like a diamond ring.

They came from the woodwork and the hopes they might,
       F   C
Re - deem themselves from poor decisions to win big.

Chorus 2

   C   Am   F   G/B
  Run, neon tiger there's a lot on your mind,
  G   C   A   A/C♯
  They'll strategize and maim you, but don't you let them tame yo
       F   E   G
You're far too pure and bold,
       F   E   G
To suffer the strain of the hangman's hold.

Bridge

 C   Caug   C6
  I don't wanna be kept, I don't wanna be caged,
           C7
I don't wanna be damned, oh hell.
 C   Caug   C6
  I don't wanna be broke, I don't wanna be saved,
           C7
I don't wanna be S.O.L.
F(♯11)   F   F6
  Give me rolling hills and tonight can be the night,
                  Fmaj7
That I stand among the thousand thrills.
 C   Caug   C6
  Mister cut me some slack, 'cause I don't wanna go back,
           C7
I want a new day and age.
 G   F
Come on girls and boys, everyone make some noise!

‖ C Caug │ C6 C7 │ C Caug │ C6 C7 ‖

Chorus 3

```
      C          Am          F              G/B
        Run, neon tiger there's a price on your head,
      G                          C      A                    A/C♯
        They'll hunt you down and gut you,   I'll never let them touch you.
          F      E     G
      A - way, a - way, oh, run,
                    F    G  E/G♯ A
      I'm begging you neon ti - ger   run.
              F    G
      Under the heat of,
              F    G
      Under the heat of,
              F    G              C
      Under the heat of the southwest sun.
```

Outro

```
      C
      Neon  tiger,
                Caug  C      Caug  C6  C7  C
      There's a lot on your   mind.
```

93

On Top

Words & Music by
Brandon Flowers, Dave Keuning, Mark Stoermer & Ronnie Vannucci

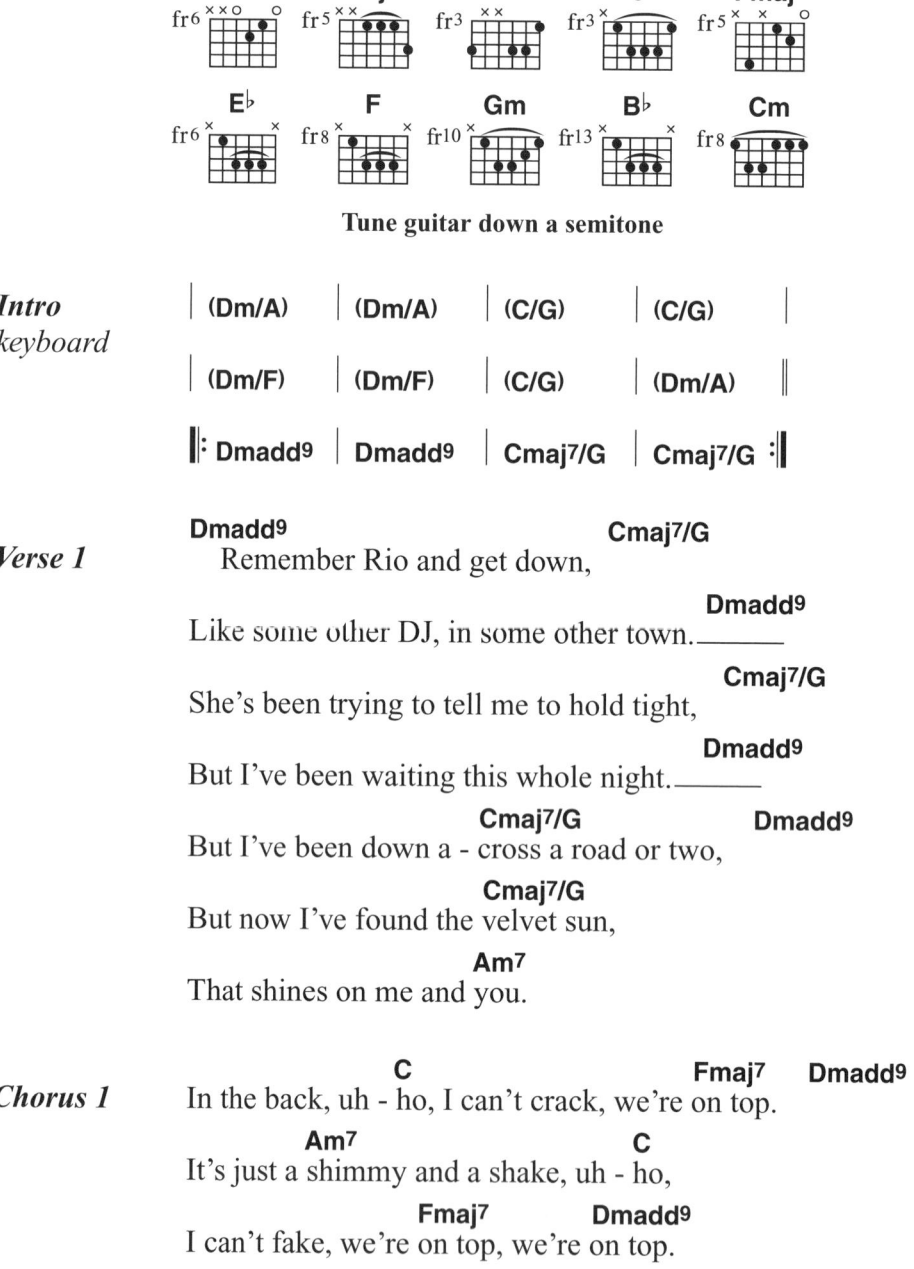

Tune guitar down a semitone

Intro
keyboard

| (Dm/A) | (Dm/A) | (C/G) | (C/G) |
| (Dm/F) | (Dm/F) | (C/G) | (Dm/A) ‖

‖: Dmadd⁹ | Dmadd⁹ | Cmaj⁷/G | Cmaj⁷/G :‖

Verse 1

Dmadd⁹   **Cmaj⁷/G**
   Remember Rio and get down,

                                                  Dmadd⁹
Like some other DJ, in some other town._____

                                              Cmaj⁷/G
She's been trying to tell me to hold tight,

                                              Dmadd⁹
But I've been waiting this whole night._____

                      Cmaj⁷/G   **Dmadd⁹**
But I've been down a - cross a road or two,

                      Cmaj⁷/G
But now I've found the velvet sun,

                  Am⁷
That shines on me and you.

Chorus 1

                  C   **Fmaj⁷**   **Dmadd⁹**
In the back, uh - ho, I can't crack, we're on top.

            Am⁷   **C**
It's just a shimmy and a shake, uh - ho,

                      Fmaj⁷   **Dmadd⁹**
I can't fake, we're on top, we're on top.

Link 1 | Dmadd⁹ | Dmadd⁹ | Cmaj⁷/G | Cmaj⁷/G ‖

Verse 2

Dmadd⁹   Cmaj⁷/G
The day is breaking, we're still here,

                            Dmadd⁹
Your body's shaking, and it's clear.

                        Cmaj⁷/G
You really need it, so let go,

                          Dmadd⁹
And let me feed it, but you know_____

                Cmaj⁷/G   Dmadd⁹
That I've been down a - cross a road or two.

               Cmaj⁷/G
But now I've found the velvet sun,

              Am⁷
That shines on me and you.

Chorus 2

                    C   Fmaj⁷   Dmadd⁹
In the back, uh - ho, I can't crack, we're on top.

          Am⁷   C
It's just a shimmy and a shake, uh - ho,

                Fmaj⁷   Dmadd⁹
I can't fake, we're on top, we're on top.

          Am⁷   C
We bring the bump to the grind, uh - ho,

                Fmaj⁷   Dmadd⁹
I don't mind, we're on top.

          Am⁷   C
It's just a shimmy and a shake, uh - ho,

                Fmaj⁷   Dmadd⁹
I can't fake, we're on top, we're on top.

Bridge 1

E♭   F   Gm   B♭   E♭
And we don't mean to satis - fy to - night,

                 F   Gm   B♭   E♭
So get your eyes off of my bride to - night.

                F   Gm   B♭
'Cause I don't need to satis - fy to - night.

         Cm   F
It's like a cigarette in the mouth,

      Cm   F
Or a   handshake in the doorway,

   Cm   F   Gm
I look at you and smile because I'm fine.

Interlude

‖: Dm(add9) | Dm(add9) | Cmaj7/G | Cmaj7/G :‖

‖: Am7 | C | Fmaj7 | Dm(add9) :‖

| Dm(add9) | N.C. ‖

Bridge 2

Eb   F   Gm   Bb   Eb
   And we don't mean to satis - fy to - night,

                    F   Gm   Bb   Eb
So get your eyes off of my bride to - night.

                         F   Gm   Bb
'Cause I don't need to satis - fy to - night.

               Cm   F
It's like a cigarette in the mouth,

         Cm   F
Or a   handshake in the doorway,

     Cm   F   Gm
I look at you and smile because I'm fine.

96

Read My Mind

Words & Music by
Brandon Flowers, Dave Keuning, Mark Stoermer & Ronnie Vannucci

D   Asus4   A   Bm   D/F♯   G   F♯7/A♯   A/C♯

Tune guitar down a semitone

Intro
‖: D | D | Asus4 | A :‖

Verse 1

     D   Asus4
I'm on the corner of main street,

                  A   D
Just tryin' to keep it in line.

                           Asus4
You say you wanna move on and,

               A
You say I'm falling be - hind.

         D   Bm D/F♯ Asus4 A
Can you read my   mind?

         D   Bm D/F♯ Asus4 A
Can you read my   mind?

Verse 2

     D   Bm   D/F♯   Asus4
I never really gave up   on,

                  A   D
Breakin' out of this two-star town.

                  Bm   D/F♯   Asus4
I got the green light, I got a little fight,

                     A
I'm gonna turn this thing a - round.

         D   Bm D/F♯ Asus4 A
Can you read my   mind?

         D   Bm D/F♯ Asus4 A
Can you read my   mind?

Pre-chorus 1
```
               G                    D
The good old days, the honest man,
               A
The restless heart, the promised land.
               G              D
A subtle kiss that no one sees,
               A
A broken wrist and a big trapeze.
```

Chorus 1
```
               G                    D
So what, I don't mind if you don't mind,
              A       F♯7/A♯   Bm
'Cause I don't shine if you don't shine.
    D/F♯     G                    A
Be - fore you go can you read my mind?
```

Verse 3
```
D                          Bm    D/F♯    Asus4
    It's funny how you just break down,
              A
Waitin' on some sign.
    D                      Bm    D/F♯    Asus4
I pull up to the front of your drive - way,
              A
With magic soakin' my spine.
                  D        Bm  D/F♯  Asus4  A
Can you read my mind?
                  D        Bm  D/F♯  Asus4  A
Can you read my mind?
```

Pre chorus 2
```
               G                  D
The teenage queen, the loaded gun,
              A
The drop dead dream, the chosen one.
               G                   D
A southern drawl and a world un - seen,
              A
A city wall and a trampoline.
```

Chorus 2
```
               G                    D
Oh well I don't mind if you don't mind,
              A       F♯7/A♯   Bm
'Cause I don't shine if you don't shine.
    D/F♯     G
Be - fore you jump,
                  A                    Bm
Tell me what you find when you read my mind.
```

Solo | **Bm** | **A** | **G** | **D A/C♯** | **Bm** |
(mind)

| **A** | **G** | **A** | **A** | **A** ‖

Pre-chorus 3

A   **G**   **D**
Slippin' in my faith until I fall,

               A
You never re - turned that call.

               G   **D**
Woman, open the door, don't let it sting,

               A
I wanna breathe that fire again.

Chorus 3   She said:

         Bm   **A**
"I don't mind if you don't mind,

           G   **D**
'Cause I don't shine if you don't shine."

        A/C♯   **Bm**
Put your back on me.

            A
Put your back on me.

            G
Put your back on me.

Outro | **D** | **Bm D/F♯** | **Asus4** | **A** ‖

D
  The stars are blazing,

     Bm **D/F♯**   **Asus4**   **A**
Like rebel diamonds cut out of the sun,

             D
Can you read my   mind?

‖: **D** | **Bm D/F♯** | **Asus4** | **A** :‖
(mind)
| **D** ‖

Romeo And Juliet

Words & Music by
Mark Knopfler

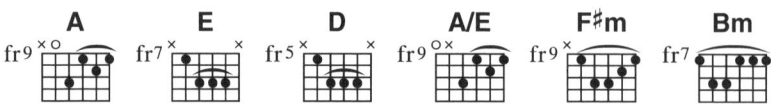

Intro | A   E | D   E | A   E | D   E |

| A   E | D   E | A/E   E | D   E ||

Verse 1
       A   F♯m   E   A

A lovestruck Romeo   sings a streetsuss sere - nade,

                          F♯m   D   E

Laying everybody low   with a lovesong that he made.

                        D   E   A

He finds a streetlight   and steps out of the shade,

                              D   E

And says something like: "you and me babe, how a - bout it?"

Verse 2
       A   E

Juliet says "Hey it's Rome - o,

F♯m   E A

You nearly gave me a heart attack."

                           E   F♯m

He's underneath the window,   she's singing:

               D   E

"Hey la, my boyfriend's back.

                                      D E   A   D

You shouldn't come around here   singing up at people like that,

                            E

Anyway what you gonna do a - bout it?"

Chorus 1

    A E   F♯m   E D
Juli - et, the dice was loaded from the start,

      A E   F♯m   E D
And I bet,   and you ex - ploded in my heart.

        A   E D F♯m   D   Bm
And I for - get, I for - get   the movie song.

When you gonna realise it was
D   E F♯m E   A
Just that the time was wrong, Juli - et?

Link 1 | A E | D E | A/E E | D E ‖
            (-et)

Verse 3

A   F♯m
   Come up on different streets,

                        E A
And both were streets of shame.

             E   F♯m
Both dirty, both mean,

                  D   E
Yes and the dream was just the same.

                         D
And I dreamed your dream for you,

    E   A   D
And now your dream is real.

How can you look at me as if I was
E
Just another one of your deals?

Verse 4

          A   E   F♯m
And you can fall for chains of silver,

                    E A
You can fall for chains of gold.

                  E   F♯m
You can fall for pretty stran - gers,

            D   E
And the promis - es they hold.

                  D E
You promised me everything,

          A   D
You promised me thick and thin, yeah.

Now you just say:

                     E
"Oh Romeo, yeah, you know I used to have a scene with him."

Chorus 2
```
         A  E                F♯m            E  D
Juli - et   when we made love you used to cry,
         A              E              F♯m        E  D
I said I love you like the stars above, I'll love you till I   die.
            A    E   D  F♯m                  D      Bm
And there's a place for   us,      you know the movie song.
```

When you gonna realise it was
```
D                    F♯m  E     A
Just that the time was wrong, Juli - et?
```

Link 2
```
| A   E  | D   E  | A/E   E | D   E  ‖
```
(-et)

Verse 5
```
A                    F♯m                      E  A
   I can't do the talk     like the talk on the T.V.
                          F♯m              D           E
And I can't do a love song     like the way it's meant to be.
                       D      E          A     D
I can't do everything    but I'd do anything for you,
                                 E
I can't do anything except be in love with you.
```

Verse 6
```
A                        F♯m                        A
   And all I do is miss you     and the way we used to be.
                          F♯m      D        E
And all do is keep the beat and     the bad company.
                          D E                A      D
And all I do is kiss you     through the bars of a rhyme.
                                 E
Juliet I'd do the stars with you   anytime.
```

Chorus 3
```
         A  E                F♯m            E  D
Juli - et   when we made love you used to cry,
         A              E              F♯m      E  D
I said I love you like the stars above, I'll love you till I   die.
            A    E   D  F♯m                  D         Bm
And there's a place for   us,      you know the movie song.
```

When you gonna realise it was
```
D                    F♯m  E      A
Just that the time was wrong, Juli - et?
```

Link 3 | A   E | D   E | A/E   E | D   E |
(-et)

                 | A   E | D   E | A/E   E | D   E ‖

Verse 7

A   F♯m   E   A

And a lovestruck Romeo   sings a streetsuss serenade,

                        F♯m   D   E

Laying everybody low   with a lovesong that he made.

                                   D   E   A

He finds a convenient street - light,   steps out of the shade,

                         D   E   D   E

Says something like: "you and me babe,   how about it?"

Outro   ‖: D | E | D | E   :‖

            | A   ‖

Ruby, Don't Take Your Love To Town

Words & Music by Mel Tillis

A⁷   Em   D   G   D/F♯

Tune guitar down a semitone

Intro
(spoken)

1, 2, a, 1, 2, 3, 4

Drums
2

Verse 1

N.C.   A⁷   Em
You've painted up your lips and rolled and curled your tinted hair,

D   G   A⁷
Ruby, are you contemplating going out some - where?

Em   A⁷   Em
The shadow on the wall tells me the sun is going down,

D   G   D/F♯ Em N.C.   D
Oh Ru - by,_____don't take your love to town.

Chorus 1

Em   D
For it wasn't me that started this whole crazy Asian war,

Em   G   A⁷
But I was proud to go and do my patriotic chores.

Em   A⁷   Em
Yes, it's true that I am not the man I used to be,

D   G   D/F♯ Em N.C.   D
Oh Ru - by, _____I still need some compa - ny.

Verse 2

D   G   A⁷   Em
It's hard to love a man whose legs are bent and para - lysed,

D   G   A⁷
And the wants and the needs of a woman your age, Ruby, I rea - lise.

Em   A⁷   Em
But it won't be long, I've heard them say, un - til I'm not around,

D   G   D/F♯ Em N.C.   D
Oh Ru - by, _____ don't take your love to town.

Verse 3

N.C.
She's leaving now 'cause I just heard the slamming of the door,

The way I know I've heard it slam one hundred times before.
      Em   A⁷   Em
And if I could move I'd get my gun and put her in the ground,
     D   G D/F♯ Em N.C.   D
Oh, Ru - by, _____don't take your love to town.
     D   G D/F♯ Em N.C.
Oh, Ru - by, _____for God sakes turn around. *(drums ad lib to fade)*

Shadowplay

Words & Music by
Ian Curtis, Peter Hook, Bernard Sumner & Stephen Morris

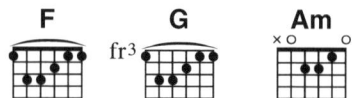

Intro   ‖: F | F G | Am | Am   :‖ *Play 4 times*

     F   G
‖: Oh, oh, oh, oh, oh, oh, oh, oh.

Am
Oh, oh, oh, oh, oh, oh, oh.

F   **G**
Oh, oh, oh, oh, oh, oh, oh, oh.

Am
Oh, oh, oh, oh, oh, oh, oh. :‖

Verse 1

(Am) F   **G**   **Am**
To the centre of the city where all roads meet, waiting for you.

        F   **G**   **Am**
To the depths of the ocean where all hopes sank, searching for you.

           F   **G** **Am**
Well, I was moving through the silence without motion, waiting for you.

        F   **G**   **Am**
In a room without a window in the corner I found truth.

Link 1   ‖: F | F G | Am | Am   :‖ *Play 4 times*

    F   G Am
       Ah._____

Verse 2

(Am) F   G Am
In the shadowplay acting out your own death, knowing no more.

                 F   G   Am
As the as - sassins all grouped in four lines, dancing on the floor.

                 F   G   Am
And with cold steel odour on their bodies, made a move to con - nect.

                 F   G   Am
But I could only stare in disbe - lief as the crowds all left.

Link 2   ‖: F | F G | Am | Am   :‖

Verse 3

(Am) F   G Am
I did everything, everything I   wanted to,

                 F   G   Am
I let them   use you for their own ends.

               F   G Am
To the centre of the city in the night, waiting for you.

               F   G Am
To the centre of the city in the night, waiting for you.

Link 3   ‖: F | F G | Am | Am   :‖ *Play 8 times*

Outro

N.C.
Oh, oh, oh, oh, oh, oh, oh, oh.

Oh, oh, oh, oh, oh, oh, oh.

Oh, oh, oh, oh, oh, oh, oh.

Show You How

Words & Music by
Brandon Flowers, Dave Keuning, Mark Stoermer & Ronnie Vannucci

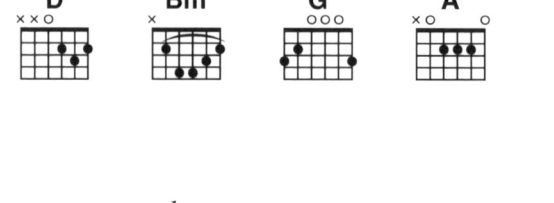

Intro

N.C.
You have one saved message.

To listen to your messages, press one, to ch-

First saved message. Message sent yesterday at 10:41 p.m.

Ha.

Verse 1

       D   **Bm**   **G**
I gotta tell ya I'll make it better,
    A   **D**   **Bm**   **G**
But I know there's somethin' I needed to say.
        A   **D**   **Bm**   **G**
When I was out, though, maybe you were better a - lone,
        A   **D** **Bm** **G**
I know I'll make it home.

Verse 2

A   **D**
She told me sweet thing,
Bm **G**   **A**
Run a labour in your shoes.
D   **Bm**   **G**
Touch me till I follow in love,
     A
I wanna help her.
D   **Bm**   **G**
Maybe we were better alone,
      A   **D** **Bm** **G** **A**
I wanna show you how.

Link 1

| D   Bm | G   A | D   Bm | G   A |

| D   Bm | G   A | D   Bm | G   A ‖

(And then we)

Verse 3

D
And then we walked out,

Bm   G
Make it made now.

A   D   Bm   G
I said I want it but I never alone.

          A
I wanna show you,

D   Bm   G
Maybe we were somethin' un - cool,

          A   D   Bm   G   A
I wanna make you sing.

Link 2

‖: D   Bm | G   A | D   Bm | G   A :‖
      Uh uh oh.   Uh uh oh.

Outro

| D   Bm | G   A | D   Bm | G   A |

| D   Bm | G   A | D   Bm/D | G/D   A/D |

| D | ‖

Smile Like You Mean It

Words & Music by
Brandon Flowers, Dave Keuning, Mark Stoermer & Ronnie Vannucci

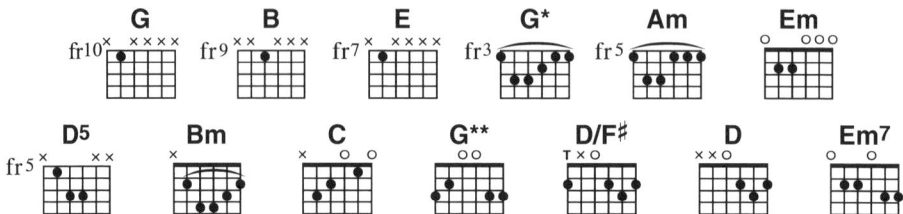

Tune down a semitone

Intro

‖: G G G G G B B E | E E E E E E E :‖ *Play 3 times*

‖: G* Am | Am | Em | Em :‖

Verse 1

G*   Am   Em
Save some face,   you know you've only got one.

G*   Am   Em | D5
Change your ways   while you're young.

G*   Am   Em | Em
Boy,   one day you'll be a man

  G* Am   Em | Em
Oh girl,   he'll help you understand.

Chorus 1

Bm   C | G** D/F# | D/F#
Smile like you mean it.

Bm   C | G** D/F# | D/F#
Smile like you mean it.

Verse 2

G*   Am   Em
Looking back   at sunsets on the Eastside,

G*   Am   Em | D5
We lost track   of the time,

G*   Am   Em | Em
Dreams   aren't what they used to be,

  G*   Am   Em | N.C.
Some   things   slide by so carelessly.

Chorus 2   As Chorus 1

Solo   ‖: D Em⁷ | Em⁷ | C | C   :‖

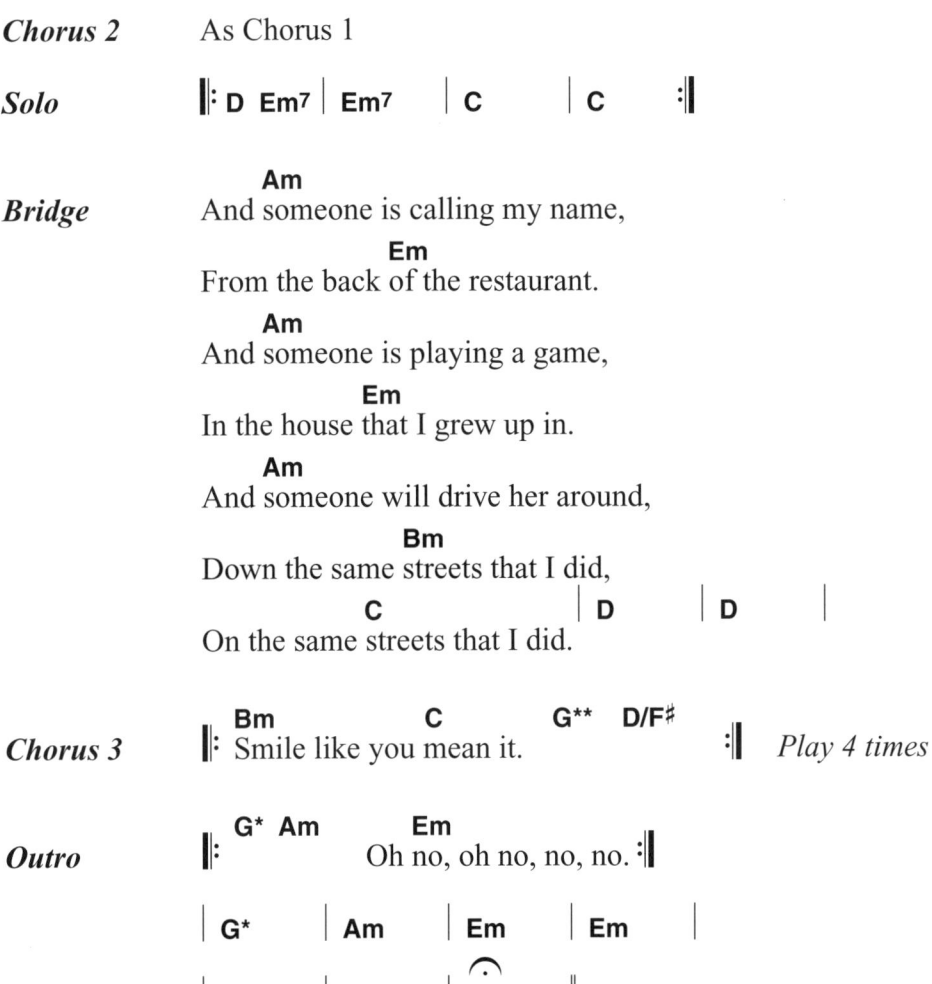

Bridge
     Am
And someone is calling my name,
           Em
From the back of the restaurant.
     Am
And someone is playing a game,
          Em
In the house that I grew up in.
     Am
And someone will drive her around,
           Bm
Down the same streets that I did,
         C | **D** | **D** |
On the same streets that I did.

Chorus 3
    Bm   **C**   **G**** **D/F♯**
‖: Smile like you mean it.   :‖ *Play 4 times*

Outro
   G* Am   **Em**
‖:   Oh no, oh no, no, no. :‖

  | **G*** | **Am** | **Em** | **Em** |

  | **G*** | **Am** | **Em** ‖

Sam's Town

Words & Music by
Brandon Flowers, Dave Keuning, Mark Stoermer & Ronnie Vannucci

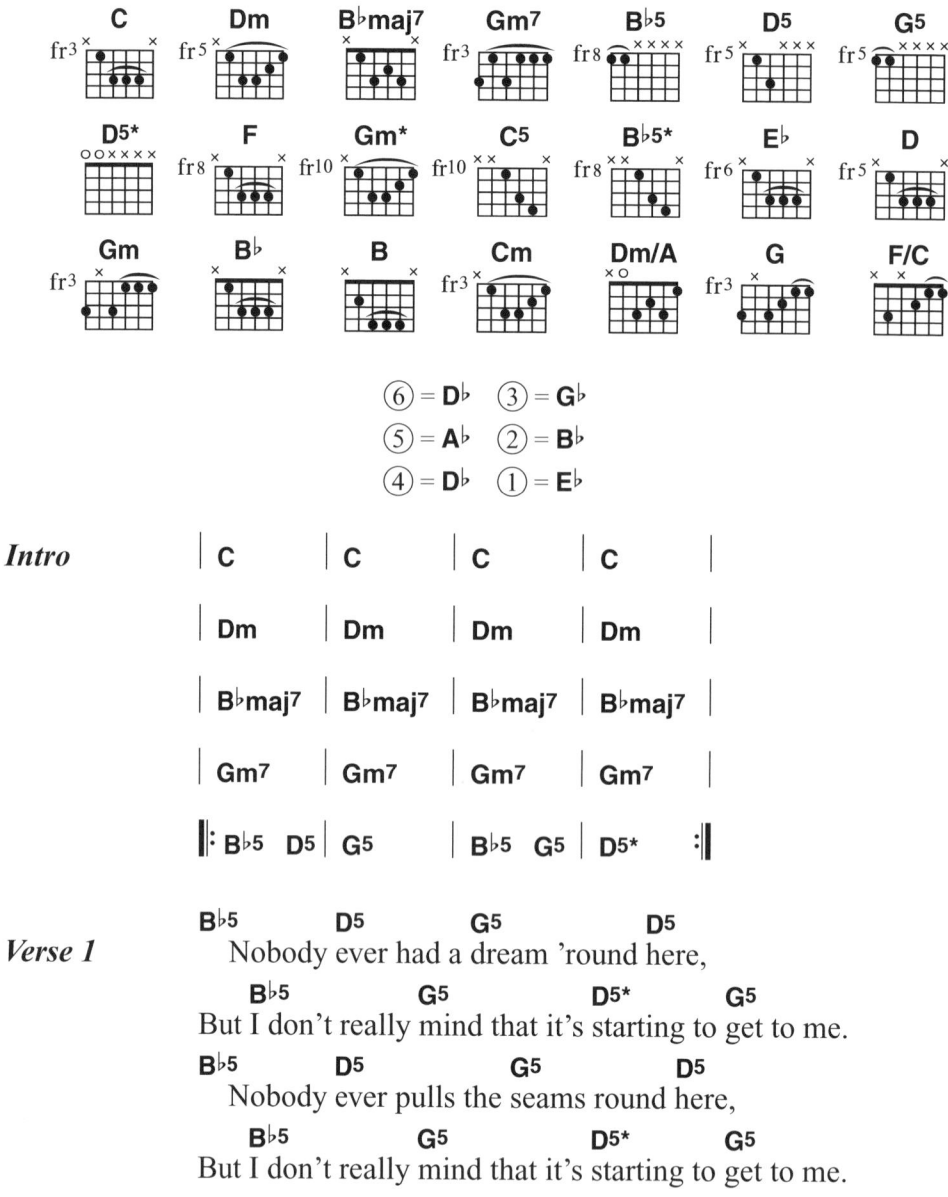

Intro

| C | C | C | C |

| Dm | Dm | Dm | Dm |

| B♭maj7 | B♭maj7 | B♭maj7 | B♭maj7 |

| Gm7 | Gm7 | Gm7 | Gm7 |

‖: B♭5 D5 | G5 | B♭5 G5 | D5* :‖

Verse 1

B♭5   D5   G5   D5
Nobody ever had a dream 'round here,

  B♭5   G5   D5*   G5
But I don't really mind that it's starting to get to me.

B♭5   D5   G5   D5
Nobody ever pulls the seams round here,

  B♭5   G5   D5*   G5
But I don't really mind that it's starting to get to me.

Pre-chorus 1

F   Gm*   C5 B♭5*
I've got this energy be - neath my feet,

  E♭   F   Dm   E♭
Like something under - ground's gonna come up and carry me.

F   Gm*   C5 B♭5
I've got this sentimental heart that beats,

  E♭   F   Dm   E♭   F
But I don't really mind and it's starting to get to me now.

Chorus 1

D   Gm
Why do you waste my time?

  Dm   E♭   F   B♭
Is the answer to the question on your mind.

   Gm   D
And I'm sick of all my judges,

  E♭   F   D
So scared of what they'll find.

   Gm   Dm
But I know that I can make it,

    E♭   F   B♭   B   Cm Cm7 D
As long as somebody takes me home every now and then.

Link 1

     B♭5   D5   G5 B♭5 G5 D5*
Oh, have you ever seen the lights?

    B♭5   D5   G5 B♭5 G5 D5*
Have you ever seen the lights?

Verse 2

B♭6   D5   G5   D5
 I took a shuttle on a shock-wave ride,

    B♭6   G5   D5*   G5
Where people on the pen pull the trigger for accolades.

B♭6   D5   G5   D5
 I took a bullet, and I looked in - side and

B♭6   G5   D5*   G5
Running through my veins an A - merican masquerade.

Pre-chorus 2

F   Gm*   C5 B♭5*
 I still re - member Grandma Dixie's wake,

  E♭   F   Dm   E♭
I'd never really known any - body to die before.

F   Gm*   C5 B♭5*
 Red, white and blue upon a birthday cake,

  E♭   F   Dm   E♭   F
My brother, he was born on the fourth of Ju - ly and that's all.

Chorus 2

    D   Gm
So why do you waste my time?

       Dm   E♭   F   B♭
Is the answer to the question on your mind.

         Gm   D
And I'm sick of all my judges,

    E♭   F   D
So scared of letting me shine.

      Gm   Dm
But I know that I can make it,

          E♭   F   B♭   Dm/A   Gm
As long as somebody takes me home._____

Bridge

   G   Cm   Dm
   Every now and then.

              E♭   F
Every now and then.

Outro

                 B♭ Dm/A Gm   E♭   Dm   F/C
You know I   see   London, I see Sam's Town,

B♭   Dm/A Gm   E♭   Dm F/C
Holds my   hand and lets my hair down.

B♭   Dm/A Gm   E♭   Dm   F/C
Rolls that   world right off my shoul - der,

B♭ Dm/A Gm   E♭   Dm   F/C   G
I   see   London, I see Sam's Town now.

‖: G | G | G | G   :‖ *Play 3 times*

| G   ‖

Somebody Told Me

Words & Music by
Brandon Flowers, Dave Keuning, Mark Stoermer & Ronnie Vannucci

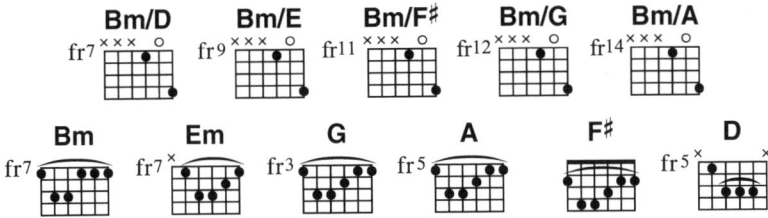

Tune guitar down a semitone

Intro 𝄆 | Bm/D | Bm/E | Bm/F♯ | Bm/G 𝄇

| Bm/F♯ Bm/G | Bm/A Bm/G | Bm/F♯ Bm/G | Bm/F♯ ‖

Verse 1

    Bm
Breaking my back just to know your name,
                                   Em   G
Seventeen tracks and I've had it with this game.
      Bm
I'm breaking my back just to know your name,

But heaven ain't close in a place like this.
                                    Em   G
Anything goes but don't blink you might miss,
        Bm
'Cause heaven ain't close in a place like this.

I said (uh) heaven ain't close in a place like this.

Pre-chorus 1

    G   A   Bm
     Bring it back down, bring it back down to - night, (hoo, hoo.)
    G   A
Never thought I'd let a rumour ruin my moonlight.

Chorus 1

N.C.   Bm   G
Well somebody told me you had a boyfriend,

               A   F♯   Bm
Who looked like a girlfriend that I had in February of last year.

           G   A   F♯ N.C.
It's not confi - dential, I've got po - tential.

Verse 2

Bm
Ready, let's roll onto something new,

                               Em   G
Taking its toll and I'm leaving without you.

        Bm
'Cause heaven ain't close in a place like this.

I said (uh) heaven ain't close in a place like this.

Pre-chorus 2

G   A   Bm
   Bring it back down, bring it back down to - night, (hoo, hoo.)
G   A
Never thought I'd let a rumour ruin my moonlight.

Chorus 2

N.C.   Bm   G
Well somebody told me you had a boyfriend,

               A   F♯   Bm
Who looked like a girlfriend that I had in February of last year.

           G   A
It's not confi - dential, I've got po - tential.

           F♯
A rushin', a rushin' around.

Bridge

G   A   Em
Pace your - self for me,——

        D   Em G
I said maybe baby please.

               Bm   A   G
But I just don't know now,——(maybe baby,)

       F♯   A
When all I wanna do is try.

Chorus 3

                   Bm   G
Well somebody told me you had a boyfriend,

             A   F♯   Bm
Who looked like a girlfriend that I had in February of last year.

               G   A
It's not confi - dential, I've got po - tential.

         F♯
A rushin', a rushin' around.

Chorus 4

                    Bm   G
‖: Well somebody told me you had a boyfriend,

             A   F♯   Bm
Who looked like a girlfriend that I had in February of last year.

               G   A
It's not confi - dential, I've got po - tential.

         F♯
A rushin', a rushin' around. :‖

| Bm   ‖

Spaceman

Words by Brandon Flowers

Muisc by Brandon Flowers, Dave Keuning, Mark Stoermer & Ronnie Vannucci

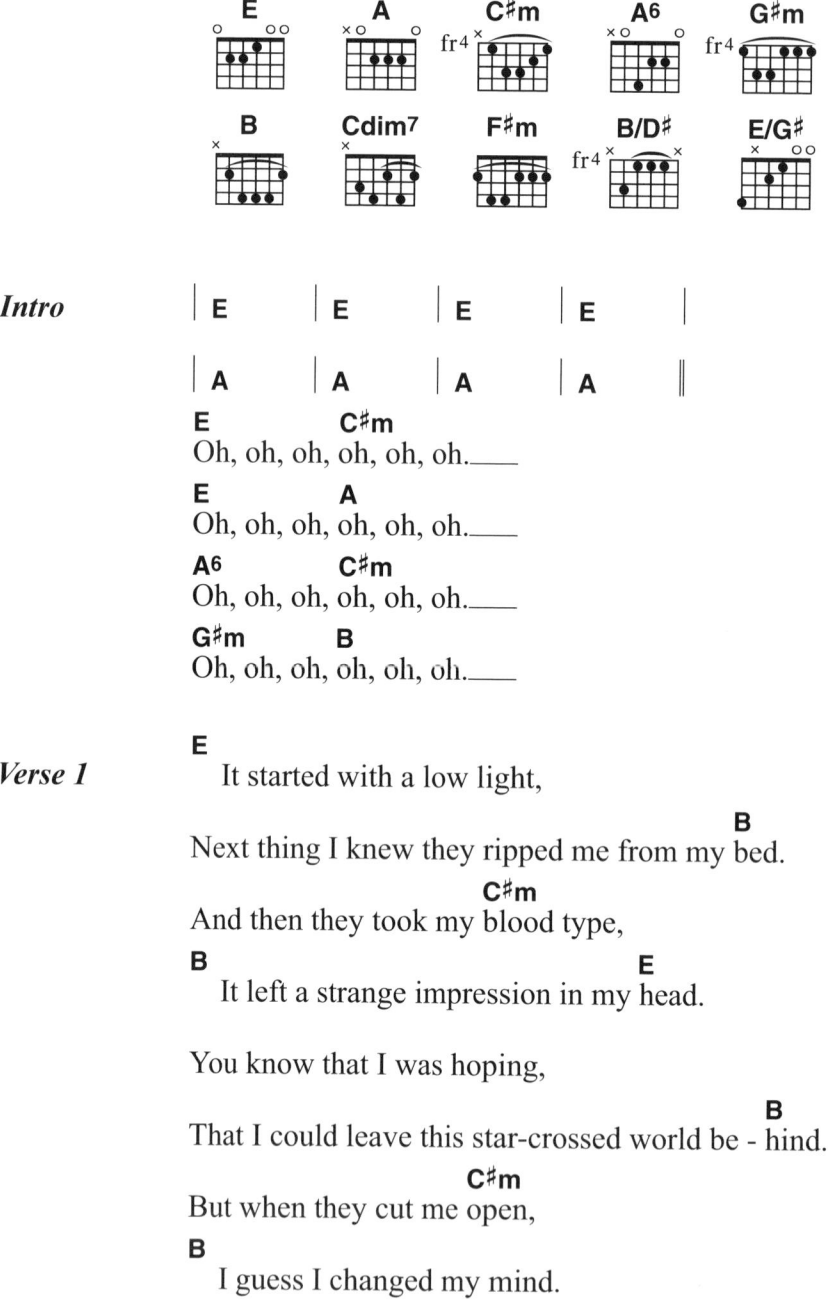

Intro

| E | E | E | E |

| A | A | A | A |

E   C♯m
Oh, oh, oh, oh, oh, oh.____

E   A
Oh, oh, oh, oh, oh, oh.____

A6   C♯m
Oh, oh, oh, oh, oh, oh.____

G♯m   B
Oh, oh, oh, oh, oh, oh.____

Verse 1

    E
It started with a low light,

                                     B
Next thing I knew they ripped me from my bed.

                      C♯m
And then they took my blood type,

B   E
It left a strange impression in my head.

You know that I was hoping,

                                   B
That I could leave this star-crossed world be - hind.

                    C♯m
But when they cut me open,

B
I guess I changed my mind.

Pre-chorus 1

    (B)   A   B   C♯m
And you know I might have just flown

         G♯m   A   B
Too far from the floor this time,

                C♯m   G♯m
'Cause they're calling me by my name,

          A
And the zipping white light beams,

    B   Cdim7   C♯m
Disregarding bombs and satel - lites.

    B
      That was the turning point,

That was one lonely night.

Chorus 1

    E   C♯m
  The song maker says, "It ain't so bad,"

    E   A
    The dream maker's gonna make you mad.

    A6   C♯m
    The spaceman says, "Everybody look down,

    G♯m   B
    It's all in your mind."

Verse 2

    E
    Well now I'm back at home, and,

                             B
I'm looking forward to this life I live.

                C♯m
You know its gonna haunt me,

    B   E
    So hesitation to this life I give.

You think you might cross over,

                                          B
You're caught between the devil and the deep blue sea.

              C♯m
You better look it over,

    B
    Before you make that leap.

Pre-chorus 2

    (B)   A   B
And you know I'm fine,

           C♯m   G♯m   A   B
But I hear those voices at night some - times.

           C♯m   G♯m
They justify my claim,

             A   B
And the public don't dwell on my transmission,

           Cdim7   C♯m
'Cause it wasn't tele - vised.

F♯m
But, it was the turning point,

B
Oh, what a lonely night.

Chorus 2   As Chorus 1

Chorus 3   As Chorus 1

Link 1   ‖: C♯m | C♯m | C♯m | C♯m :‖

Bridge

    C♯m
      My global position systems are vocally addressed,

E   C♯m
    They say the Nile used to run from East to West.

                      A B   A
They say the Nile used to run   from East to West.

      G♯m   C♯m   B   E   F♯m   A B
I'm fine, but I hear those voices at night sometime.

Chorus 4

    E   B/D♯
    The song maker says, "It ain't so bad,"

A   E/G♯
    The dream maker's gonna make you mad.

B   C♯m
    The spaceman says, "Everybody look down,

A   B
    It's all in your mind."

cont.

```
E                          B/D♯
The song maker says, "It ain't so bad,"
A                              E/G♯
The dream maker's gonna make you mad.
B                      C♯m
The spaceman says, "Everybody look down,
A  B                (E)
   It's all in your mind."
```

Outro

```
| E      | C♯m   | E      | A        |

| A⁶     | C♯m   | G♯m    ‖

B              E        C♯m  E  A
  It's all in my   mind.
                A⁶     C♯m  G♯m  B
It's all in my mind.

‖: E     | C♯m   | E      | A        |

| A⁶     | C♯m   | G♯m    | B       :‖  Repeat to fade
```

Sweet Talk

Words & Music by
Brandon Flowers, Dave Keuning, Mark Stoermer & Ronnie Vannucci

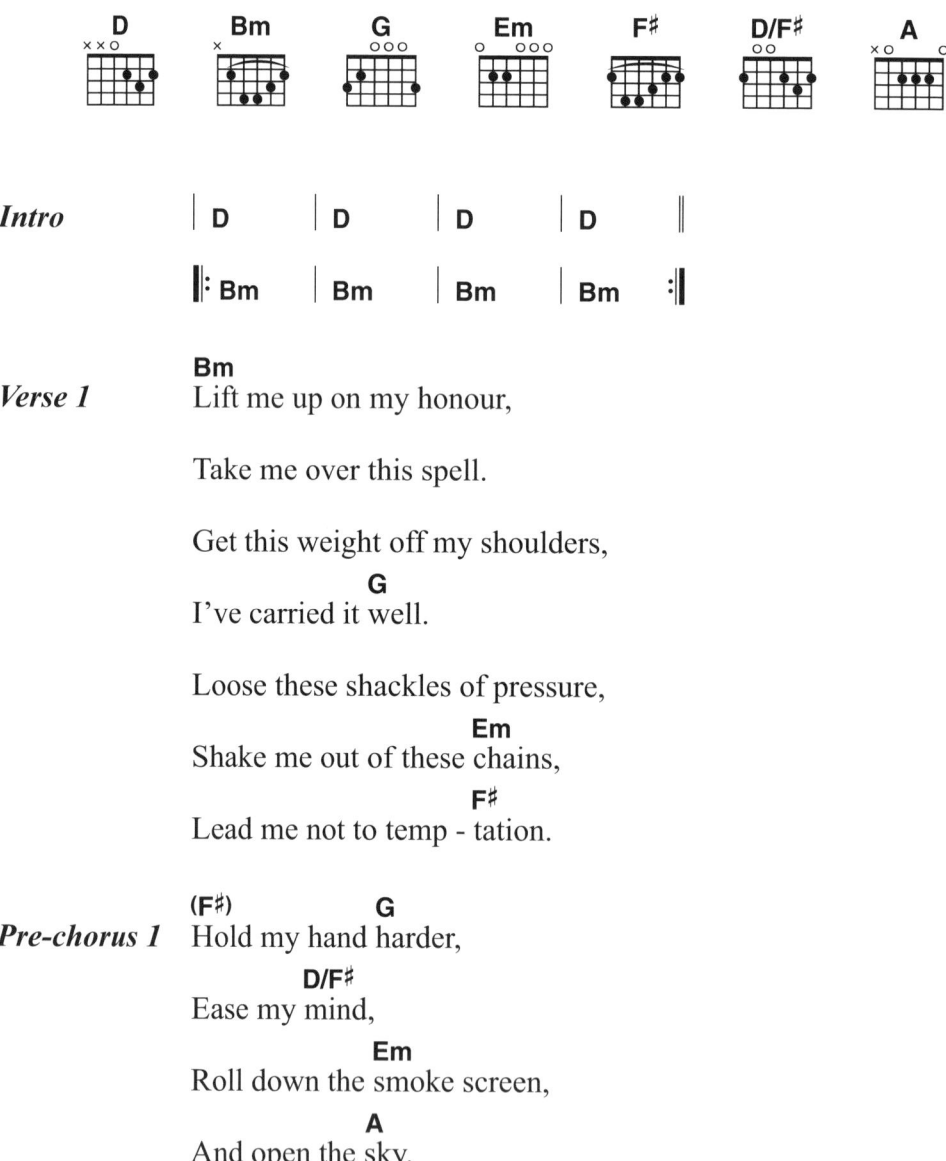

Intro | D | D | D | D   ‖

‖: Bm | Bm | Bm | Bm   :‖

Verse 1

Bm
Lift me up on my honour,

Take me over this spell.

Get this weight off my shoulders,
G
I've carried it well.

Loose these shackles of pressure,
Em
Shake me out of these chains,
F♯
Lead me not to temp - tation.

Pre-chorus 1

(**F♯**)   **G**
Hold my hand harder,
D/F♯
Ease my mind,
Em
Roll down the smoke screen,
A
And open the sky.

Chorus 1

    (A)   **D**
Let me fly,

Man, I need a release from,

This troublesome mind.

Fix my feet when they're stumbling,
                            G
And well, you know it hurts sometimes,
                       A
You know it's gonna bleed sometimes.

Link 1   ‖: Bm | Bm | Bm | Bm :‖

Verse 1

Bm
Dig me out from this thorn tree,

Help me bury my shame.

Keep my eyes from the fire,
                      G
They can't handle the flame.

Grace cut out from my brothers,
                    Em **G**
When most of them fell,
              Em   **A**
I carry it well.

Chorus 2

    (A)   **D**
Let me fly,

Man, I need a release from,

This troublesome mind.

Fix my feet when they're stumbling,
                    G
I guess you know it hurts sometimes,
                     A
You know it's gonna bleed sometimes.

Chorus 3

(A)   D
Now hold on,

I'm not looking for sweet talk,

I'm looking for time.

Top a tower and sleep walk,
                    G
Brother, 'cause it hurts sometimes,
                      A
You know it's gonna bleed sometimes.
          (D/F♯)
Hold on.

Link 2

| D/F♯ | D | G | G | |
| Em | Em | A | A | ‖

Bridge

(A)   D
You know its gonna hurt sometimes,
          Bm
When you call me.
        G   A
Hold on.
        D   Bm
Hold on.
        G   A
Hold on.

Outro

(A)   D
I'm gonna climb that symphony home and make it mine,

Let his resonance light my way.
                 G
See, all these pessimistic sufferers tend to drag me down,
A   D
So I could use it to shelter what good I've found.

This Is Your Life

Words by Brandon Flowers
Music by Brandon Flowers, Dave Keuning, Mark Stoermer & Ronnie Vannucci

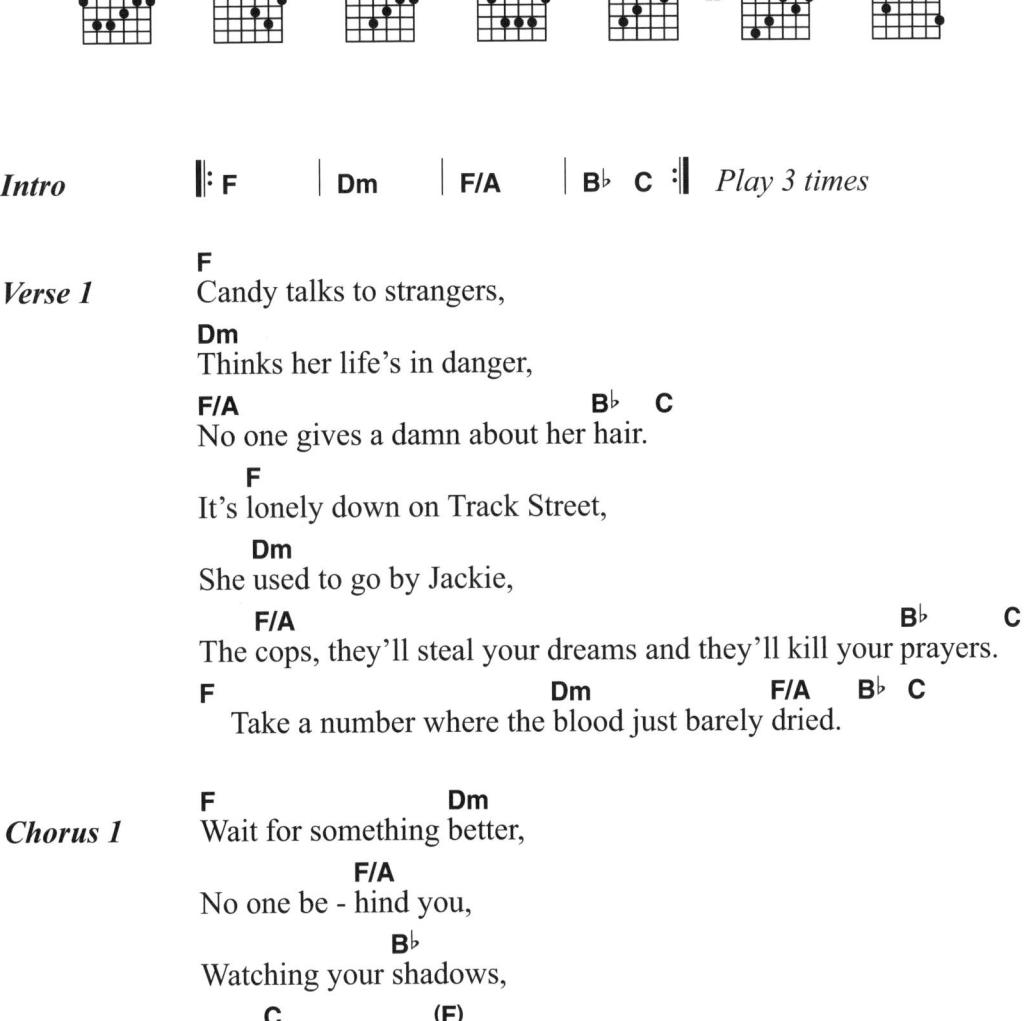

Intro   ‖: F | Dm | F/A | B♭ C :‖ *Play 3 times*

Verse 1

F
Candy talks to strangers,

Dm
Thinks her life's in danger,

F/A   B♭   C
No one gives a damn about her hair.

            F
It's lonely down on Track Street,

      Dm
She used to go by Jackie,

        F/A   B♭   C
The cops, they'll steal your dreams and they'll kill your prayers.

F   Dm   F/A   B♭ C
    Take a number where the blood just barely dried.

Chorus 1

      F   Dm
Wait for something better,

              F/A
No one be - hind you,

                  B♭
Watching your shadows,

        C   (F)
This feeling won't go.

Link 1   ‖ F | Dm | F/A | B♭ C ‖

Verse 2
F
Crooked wheels keep turning,
Dm
Children, are you learning?
     F/A   **B♭** **C**
Ac - climatize but don't you lose the plot.
   F
A history of blisters,
     Dm
Your brothers and your sisters,
F/A   **B♭** **C**
Somewhere in the pages we for - got.

Bridge 1
B♭
   Take a number Jackie,
        F   **B♭**
Where the blood just barely dried,
   E♭   **C**
You know I'm on your side.

Chorus 2
F   **Dm**
Wait for something better,
       F/A
No one be - hind you,
      B♭
Watching your shadows.
   C   **F**   **Dm**
You gotta be stronger than the sto - ry,
      F/A
Don't let it blind you,
    B♭
Rivers are shallow,
   C
This feeling won't go.

Bridge 2

F/A   B♭
And the sky is full of dreams,

C   Dm
But you don't know how to fly.

G/B   B♭
I don't have a simple an - swer,

                 C
But I know that I could an - swer,

        F   Dm F/A B♭ C
With something better.

Outro

F Dm F/A B♭   C   F   Dm F/A B♭
               This feeling won't go.

C
Wait for it.

F   Dm
Wait for it.

          F/A
Wait for it.

         B♭ C
Wait for it.

‖: F | Dm | F/A | B♭ C :‖ F   ‖

This River Is Wild

Words & Music by
Brandon Flowers, Dave Keuning, Mark Stoermer & Ronnie Vannucci

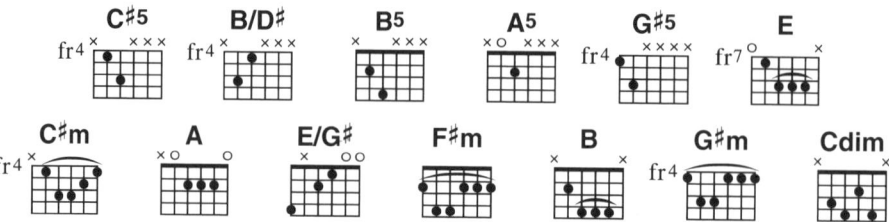

Tune guitar down a semitone

Intro | C#5 B/D# |

| B5 C#5 A5 | A5   B5 | G#5   A5 C#5| C#5 B/D# |

| B5 C#5 A5 | A5   B5 | G#5   A5 E | E |

Verse 1
    E
Leaves are falling down on the beautiful ground,
       C#m
I heard a story from the man in red.
        E
He said the leaves are falling down, such a beautiful sound,
      C#m
Son, I think you better go ahead.

Verse 2
       E
But you always hold your head up high,
B5   **C#m**
'Cause it's a long, long, long way down.
       B5 **E**
This town was meant for passing through, but it ain't nothing new,
     B5   **C#m**
Now go and show them that the world stayed round.
B   **A**   **E/G#**
But it's a long, long, long way down.

Link 1 | F#m | C#m | E |

           | A | E/G# | B ||
                                 (You better)

                   B   E
Verse 3   You better run for the hills before they burn,
                   B⁵   C#m
            Listen to the sound of the world don't watch it turn.
                      B⁵   F#m   G#m
            I just want to show you what I know,
                                       A   B
            And catch you when the current lets you go.

                                 E
Bridge 1 Or should I just get along with myself,
                   B   C#m
            I never did get along with ev'rybody else.
                   B   E
            I've been trying hard to do what's right,
                      B   C#m   B   A
            But you know I could stay here all night,
                                    E/G#   F#m
            And watch the clouds fall from the sky.
                      B   E B C#m
            This river is wild.
                         B
            This river is wild.

Link 2 | E | E   B | C#m | C#m   B||

                 E
Verse 4   Run for the hills before they burn,
                   B⁵   C#m   B⁵
            Listen to the sound of the world don't watch it turn but shake a little.
            E   B⁵
            Sometimes I'm nervous when I talk, I shake a little.
            C#m
            Sometimes I hate the line I walk.
                      B⁵   F#m   G#m
            I just want to show you what I know,
                                       A   B
            And catch you when the current lets you go.

129

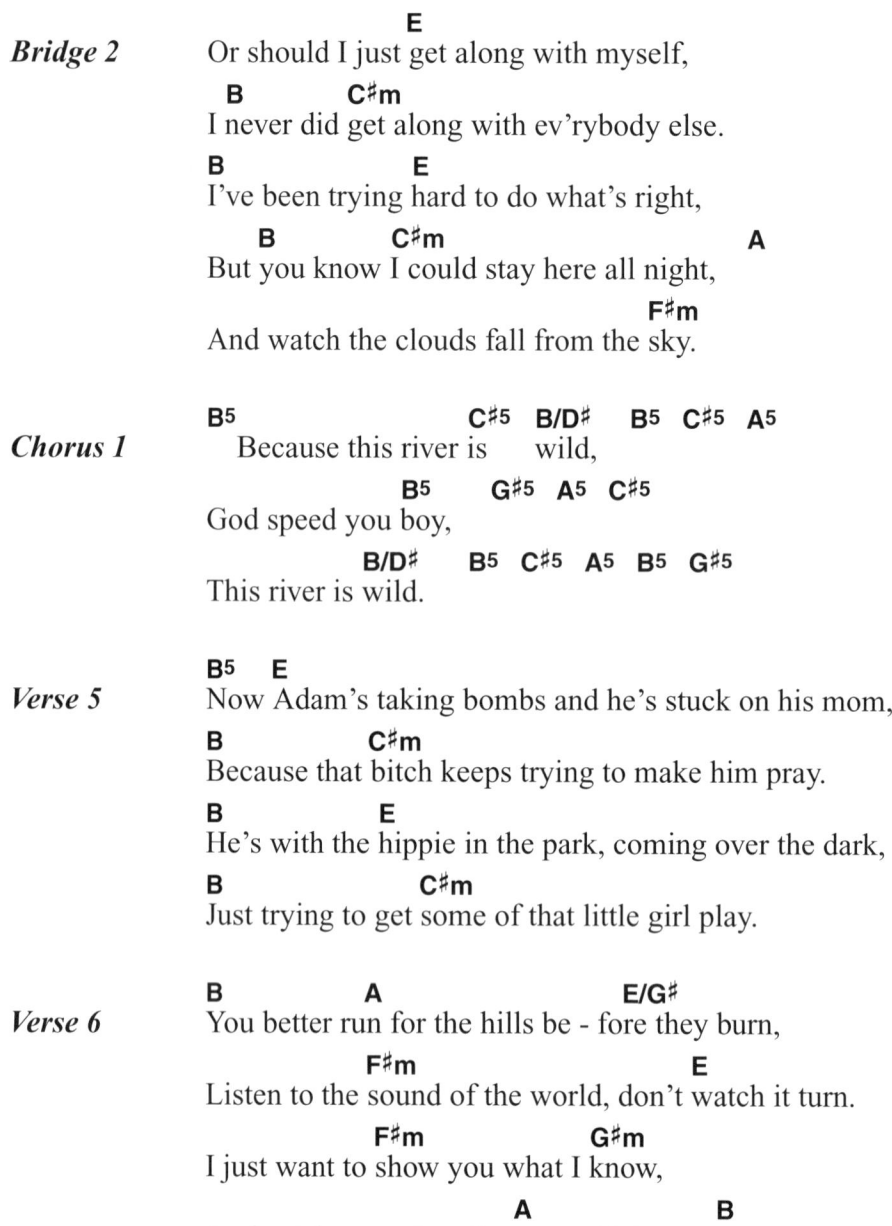

Bridge 2

                  E
Or should I just get along with myself,

  B   **C♯m**
I never did get along with ev'rybody else.

B   **E**
I've been trying hard to do what's right,

  B   **C♯m**   **A**
But you know I could stay here all night,

                               F♯m
And watch the clouds fall from the sky.

Chorus 1

B5   **C♯5** **B/D♯**   **B5** **C♯5** **A5**
  Because this river is   wild,

              B5   **G♯5** **A5** **C♯5**
God speed you boy,

          B/D♯   **B5** **C♯5** **A5** **B5** **G♯5**
This river is wild.

Verse 5

B5   **E**
Now Adam's taking bombs and he's stuck on his mom,

B   **C♯m**
Because that bitch keeps trying to make him pray.

B   **E**
He's with the hippie in the park, coming over the dark,

B   **C♯m**
Just trying to get some of that little girl play.

Verse 6

B   **A**   **E/G♯**
You better run for the hills be - fore they burn,

            F♯m   **E**
Listen to the sound of the world, don't watch it turn.

            F♯m   **G♯m**
I just want to show you what I know,

                  A   **B**
And catch you when the current lets you go.

Bridge 3

               E
Or should I get along with myself,
       A   **E/G♯**
I never did get along with ev'ry - body else.
               B   **C♯m**
I've been trying hard to do what's right,
                 E   **A**
But you know I could stay here   all night,
                           F♯m   **B** **A**
And watch the clouds fall from the sky.
                      B
And pay this hell in me to - night.

Chorus 2

               C♯5 **B/D♯**   **B5** **C♯5** **A5**
Because this river is   wild,
              B5   **G♯5** **A5** **C♯5**
God speed you boy,
             B/D♯   **B5** **C♯5** **A5** **B5** **G♯5** **B5** **C♯5**
This river is wild.

Chorus 3

             B/D♯   **B5** **C♯5** **A5**
This river is wild,
              B5   **G♯5** **A5** **C♯5**
God speed you boy,
             B/D♯   **B5** **C♯5** **A5** **B5** **G♯5**
This river is wild.

Outro

B5   **E**   **A**
Now the cars are everywhere, face in dust at the fairground.
                                      E/G♯   **B**
I don't think I ever seen so many headlights.
                       Cdim **C♯m**
But there's something pulling me.
       E
The circus and the crew,
             B/D♯
Well they're just passing through,
      C♯m   **B**   **A**
Making sure the merry still goes round.
         B   **E**
But it's a long, long, long way down.

Tidal Wave

Words & Music by
Brandon Flowers, Dave Keuning, Mark Stoermer & Ronnie Vannucci

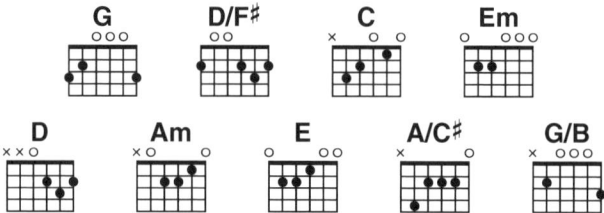

Tune guitar down a semitone

Intro | G | G | G | G   ‖

Verse 1
G   D/F♯
He's always trouble with his non - com - placence,
            C   Em
And shotgun eyes, shotgun eyes.
            C   Em   C   D
His subtlety is mystery,   not like the other guys.
            G   D/F♯
She's always taken by his repu - tation,
            C   Em
He's so bad, he's so bad.
            C   D   Em   (C)
On Saturday night they're running for the shadows.

Link 1 | C | G | D | D   ‖

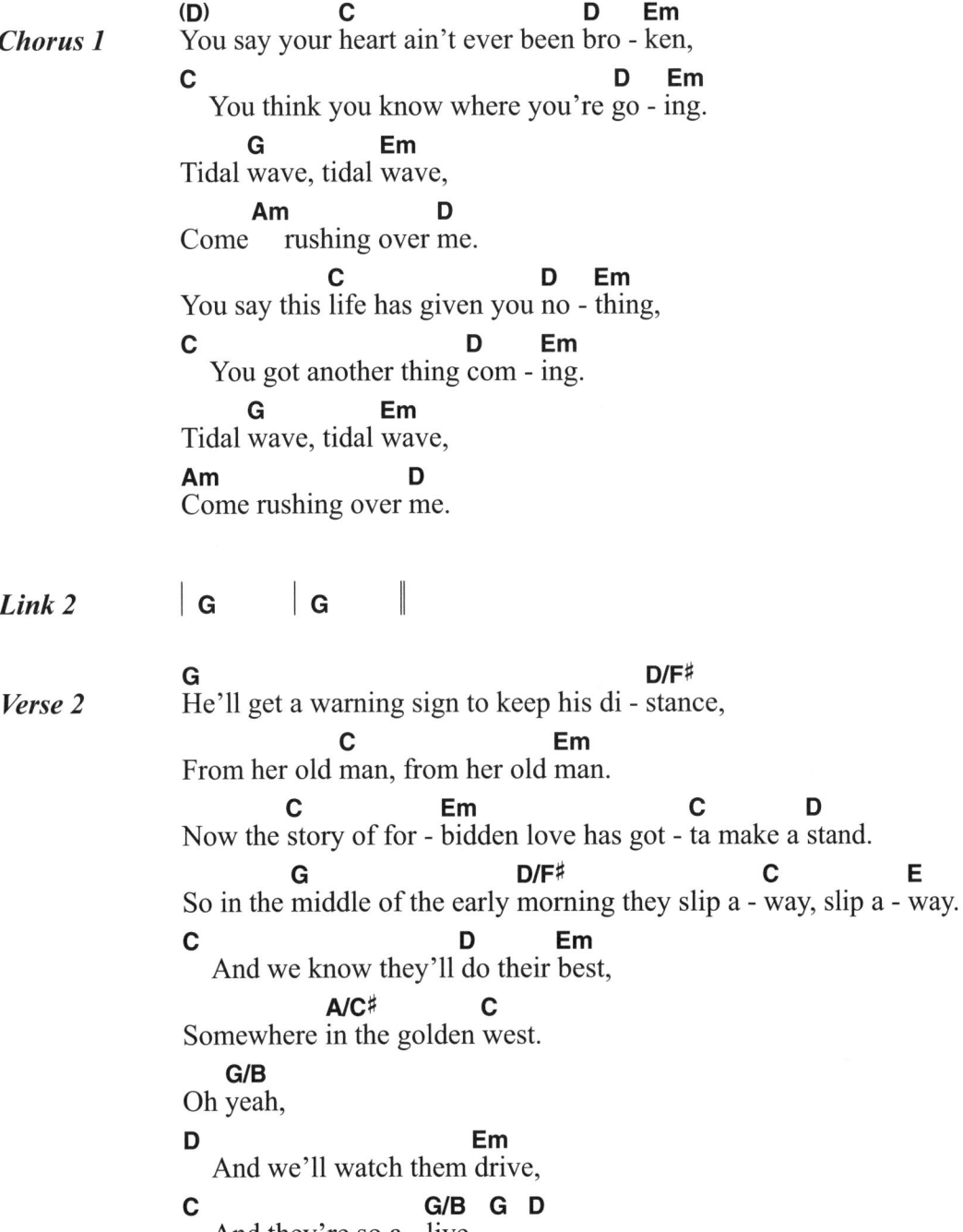

Chorus 1

   (D)   **C**   **D**   **Em**
You say your heart ain't ever been bro - ken,

C   **D**   **Em**
  You think you know where you're go - ing.

      G   **Em**
Tidal wave, tidal wave,

     Am   **D**
Come rushing over me.

         C   **D**   **Em**
You say this life has given you no - thing,

C   **D**   **Em**
  You got another thing com - ing.

      G   **Em**
Tidal wave, tidal wave,

Am   **D**
Come rushing over me.

Link 2 | **G** | **G**   ‖

Verse 2

G   **D/F♯**
He'll get a warning sign to keep his di - stance,

         C   **Em**
From her old man, from her old man.

      C   **Em**   **C**   **D**
Now the story of for - bidden love has got - ta make a stand.

       G   **D/F♯**   **C**   **E**
So in the middle of the early morning they slip a - way, slip a - way.

C   **D**   **Em**
  And we know they'll do their best,

       A/C♯   **C**
Somewhere in the golden west.

  G/B
Oh yeah,

D   **Em**
  And we'll watch them drive,

C   **G/B** **G** **D**
  And they're so a - live.

Chorus 2

    (D)   C   D   Em
You say your heart ain't ever been bro - ken,

C   D   Em
   You think you know where you're go - ing.

      G   Em
Tidal wave, tidal wave,

       Am   D
Come   rushing over me.

              C   D   Em
You say this life has given you no - thing,

C   D   Em
   You got another thing com - ing.

      G   Em
Tidal wave, tidal wave,

Am   D
Come rushing over me.

Tidal wave.

Link 3 | Em | Em | C | C | D | D   ‖

Outro

(D)   C   G/B
These tidal waves are caught off track,

D   Em
   Come tomorrow 'cause I can't go back.

C   Em
   We're all together, can't you see,

Am   D
   Tidal wave gonna cover me.

       C   G/B
These tidal waves are caught off track,

D   Em
   Come tomorrow 'cause I can't go back.

C   Em
   Come together, can't you see,

Am   D
   Tidal wave gonna cover me,

C D   Em
   Cover me.

C D   Em
   I can't go back,

C Em   G D
   Can't you see.

Tranquilize

Words & Music by
Brandon Flowers, Dave Keuning, Mark Stoermer & Ronnie Vannucci

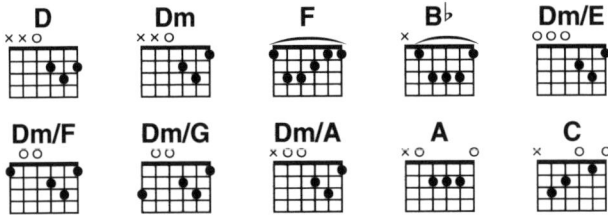

Tune guitar down a semitone

Intro   ‖: D | Dm | Dm | Dm :‖

Verse 1
Dm
Time it tells living in my home town,

Wedding bells they begin easy.

Live it down, baby don't talk that much,

Baby knows, but baby don't tease me.
F
  In the park we could go walking,
B♭
Drown in the dark or we could go sailing
Dm
  On the sea.

Verse 2
Dm
Always here, always on time,

Close call, was it love or was it just easy?

Money talks when people need shoes and socks,

Steady boys, I'm thinking she needs me.
F   **B♭**
I was just sipping on something sweet,

I don't need political process.

Pre-chorus 1

Dm   Dm/E
   I got this feeling that they're gonna break down the door,

Dm/F   Dm/G   Dm/A
   I got this feeling they they're gonna come back for more.

Dm   Dm/E
   See I was thinking that I lost my mind,

Dm/F   Dm/G   Dm/A
   But it's been getting to me all this time

       A
And it don't stop dragging me down.

Chorus 1

F   C   Dm   B♭
Silently re - flection turns my world to stone,

F   C   Dm   A
Patiently cor - rection leaves us all a - lone.

   B♭   C
And sometimes I'm a travel man,

       Dm   C   B♭ C
But to - night this engine's fail - ing.

And I   still hear the child - ren play - ing.

Verse 3

Dm
   Kick the can, kick the can, skip and blackjack,

Steal a car and ring a round-rosey,

Rock and roll, candyman, boogeyman,

Run away and give me your sneakers.

Verse 4

Dm
Acid rain, when Abel looked up at Cain,

We began the weeping and wailing.

A hurried high from pestilence, pills and pride,

It's a shame, we could of gone sailing.

F
   But heaven knows,

          B♭
Heaven knows every - thing,

Tranquilize.

Pre-chorus 2   As Pre-chorus 1

Chorus 2

    F   C   Dm   B♭
Silently re - flection turns my world to stone,

    F   C   Dm   A
Patiently cor - rection leaves us all a - lone.

      B♭   C
And sometimes I'm a travel man,

        Dm   C B♭ C
But to - night this engine's fail - ing.

F E   D   C D   C B♭   A
3fr 2fr 0 3fr 0   3fr 1fr   0
④ ④ ④ ⑤ ④   ⑤ ⑤   ⑤
And I still hear the child - ren play - ing.

C   A   G   F B♭   A   G   E
3fr 0 3fr 1fr 1fr 0 3fr 0
⑤ ⑤ ⑥   ⑥ ⑤   ⑤ ⑥ ⑥ F
Dead beat danc - ers come to us and stay.

Outro

    F   Dm
  'Cause I don't care where you've been,

      C   F/A
And I don't care what you've seen.

        Dm   Gm
We're the ones who still be - lieve,

          C   F
And we're looking for a page.

        C/E   Dm
In that lifeless book of hope,

         C   F/A
Where a dream might help you cope

        Dm   Gm
With the Bushes and the bombs,

      C   F
Ah, ha, tranqui - lized.

Uncle Jonny

Words & Music by
Brandon Flowers, Dave Keuning, Mark Stoermer & Ronnie Vannucci

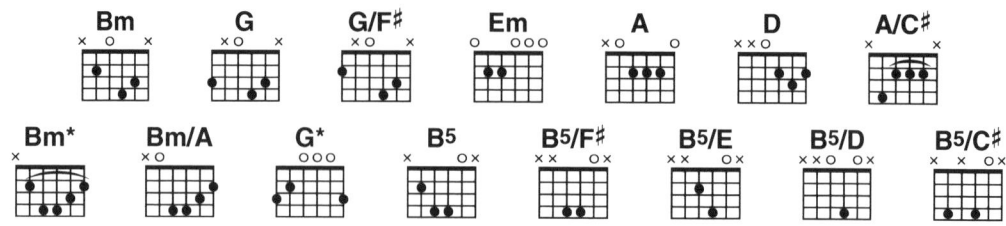

Tune guitar down a semitone

Intro

| Bm | Bm | Bm | Bm |

| Bm | Bm | Bm | G G/F# :|

Verse 1

         Bm
When ev'rybody else refrained,
              G   **G/F#**
My uncle Jonny did co - caine.
           Bm
He's con - vinced himself right in his brain,
                   G
That it helps to take away the pain.
G/F# **Bm**
Hey,   Jonny.
G   **G/F#**
  Hey what you say Jonny?

Verse 2

       Bm
I wanna go out tonight,
                   G   **G/F#**
Come a little closer to the city lights.
        Bm
Levi - tation ain't your only friend,
               G   **G/F#**
Levitation coming back a - gain.

	G G/F♯
Chorus 1	You feel a burning in your body core,

        G   **G/F♯**

Chorus 1   You feel a burning in your body core,

        Em
It's a yearning that you can't ignore.

        Bm
And I wanna go out tonight,

          A
S - s - s - superman and hold on tight.

          G   **A**
He's con - vinced himself right in his brain,

        D   **A/C♯**   **Bm***
That it helps to take a - way the pain.

Bm/A **G***   **A**
Hey,   Jonny.

Hey what you say Jonny?

Link 1	| Bm	| Bm	| Bm	| G G/F♯ ||

        Bm

Verse 3   My appetite ain't got no heart,

                        G   **G/F♯**
I said my appetite ain't got no heart.

         Bm
Shocking people when you feel that pull,

                       G   **G/F♯**
Shock 'em, drop 'em when you know it's full.

          G   **G/F♯**

Chorus 2   I feel a burning in my body core,

        Em
It's a yearning that you can't ignore.

     Bm
I gotta go out tonight,

             A
Hey Jonny I got faith in you man.

I mean it, it's gonna be all right.

          G   **A**
He's con - vinced himself right in his brain,

        D   **A/C♯**   **Bm***
That it helps to take a - way the pain.

Bm/A **G***   **A**
Hey,   Jonny.

Hey what you say Jonny?

Bridge

D   A/C♯   Bm*
  Tell us what's going on,

      Bm/A   G* A
Feels like everything's wrong.

              D
Hey what you say Jonny?

    A/C♯ Bm*
If the future is real,

     Bm/A   G* A
Jonny, you've got to heal.

Hey what you say Jonny?

Link 2 ‖: Bm | Bm | Bm | G G/F♯ :‖

       B5
Outro When everybody else refrained,

    B5/F♯   B5/E B5/D B5/C♯ Bm
My uncle Jonny did co - caine.

When You Were Young

Words & Music by
Brandon Flowers, Dave Keuning, Mark Stoermer & Ronnie Vannucci

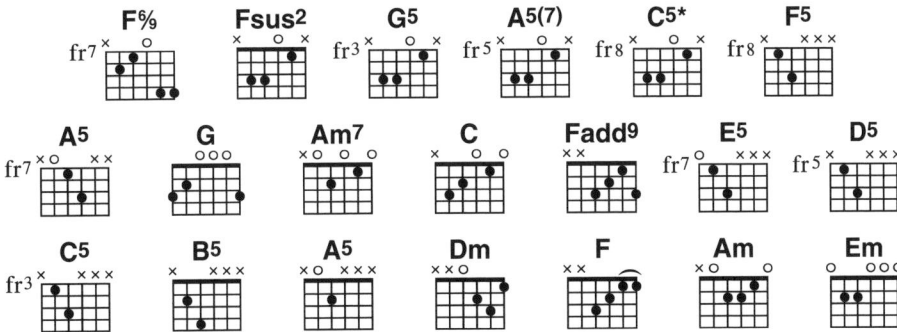

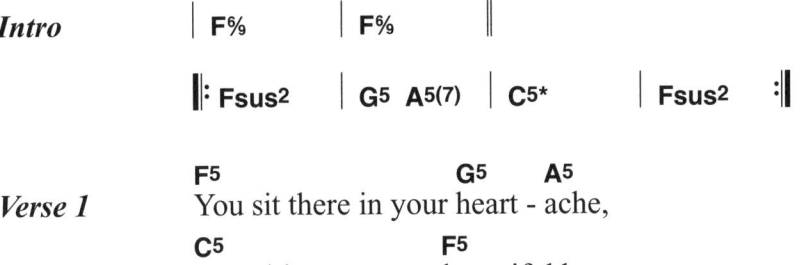

Tune guitar down a semitone

Intro
|| : F% | F% || ||

|| : Fsus2 | G5 A5(7) | C5* | Fsus2 :||

Verse 1

   F5   G5   A5
You sit there in your heart - ache,

   C5   F5
     Waiting on some beautiful boy to,

                          G5   A5
To save you from your old ways.

   C5
     You play forgiveness,

       F5
Watch it now, here he comes!

Pre-chorus 1

     Fsus2   G   Am7
He doesn't look a thing like Je - sus,

                 C
But he talks like a gentleman,

Fadd9
Like you imagined.

Chorus 1

         Fsus2   G5   A5(7) C5* Fsus2
When you were young.

Verse 2

F5
Can we climb this mountain?

G5   **A5**
 I don't know,

C5   **F5**
 Higher now than ever before,

                              G5   **A5**
I know we can make it if we take it slow.

C5
 That's takin' easy,

    F5
Ea - sy now, watch it go!

Pre-chorus 2

        Fsus2   **G**   **Am7**
We're burning down the highway sky - line,

        C   **Fadd9**
On the back of a hurricane that started turning,

Chorus 2

      Fsus2   **G5**   **A5(7) C5* Fsus2**
When you were young.

Fsus2   **G5**   **A5(7) C5* Fsus2**
 When you were young.

Bridge

    Fsus2   **G**
 And sometimes you close your eyes,

   Am7   **C**   **Fadd9**
And see the place where you used to live,

    Fsus2 G5
When you   were young.

Instr.

‖: **Fsus2** | **G5 A5(7)** | **C5*** | **Fsus2** :‖

| **F5 E5 D5** | **C5 B5 A5** | **G5** | **G5**   ‖

Middle 8

      Dm
They say the devil's water, it ain't so sweet,

    F   **Am**
You don't have to drink right now,

Em   **Am**
 But you can dip your feet,

G
 Every once in a little while.

Link   ‖: **Fsus2** | **G5 A5(7)** | **C5** | **Fsus2**   :‖

F5   **G5**   **A5**

Verse 3   You sit there in your heart - ache,

C5   **F5**

Waiting on some beautiful boy to,

                G5 A5

To save you from your old ways.

C5

You play forgiveness,

    F5

Watch it now, here he comes!

       Fsus2   **G**   **Am7**

Pre-chorus 3   He doesn't look a thing like Je - sus,

     C

But he talks like a gentleman,

Fadd9

Like you imagined.

      Fsus2   **G5**   **A5(7)**

Chorus 3   When you were young.

C5   **Fsus2**

Talks like a gentlemen, like you imagined,

     Fsus2   **G5**   **A5(7) C5 Fsus2**

When you were young.

                 G5 A5(7) C5

I said he doesn't look a thing like Je - sus,

Fsus2   **G5 A5(7) C5**

He doesn't look a thing like Je - sus,

Fsus2

But more than you'll ever know.

Outro | **F5 E5 D5** | **C5 B5 A5** | **G5**   ‖

143

Under The Gun

Words & Music by
Brandon Flowers, Dave Keuning, Mark Stoermer & Ronnie Vannucci

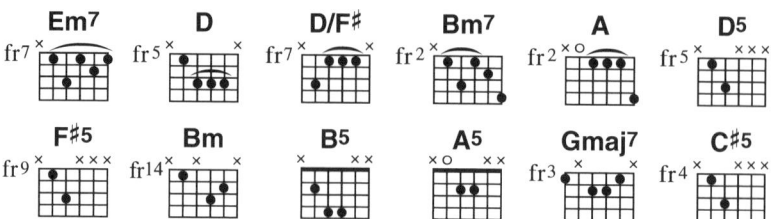

Tune guitar down a semitone

Verse 1
    N.C.   Em⁷   D
She's got her halo and wings hidden under his eyes,
            Em⁷   D/F♯
But she's an angel for sure, she just can't stop telling lies.
            Em⁷   D
But it's too late for his love already caught in a trap,
            Em⁷   D/F♯
His angel's kiss was a joke and she is not coming back.

Pre-chorus 1
                     Bm⁷
Because heaven sends and heaven takes,
           A   Bm⁷
Crashing cars in his brain keep him tied up to a dream.
           A
And only she can set him free, and then he says to me:

Chorus 1
  D5   F♯5   Bm
"Kill me now, kill me now, kill me now, kill me   now.
  D5   F♯5   Bm
Kill me now, kill me now, kill me now, kill me   now."

Verse 2
                         Em⁷   D
Yeah, she's got a criminal mind, he's got a reason to pray,
            Em⁷   D/F♯
His life is under the gun, he's got to hold every day.
              Em⁷   D
Now he just wants to wake up yeah, just to prove it's a dream,
            Em⁷   D/F♯
'Cause she's an angel for sure, but that remains to be seen.

Pre-chorus 2   As Pre-chorus 1

Chorus 2   As Chorus 1

Bridge

B5   **A5**   **B5**
Stupid on the streets of London, James Dean in the rain.
                A5   **Gmaj7**
Without her   it's not the same, the same, the same,
           A
But it's alright.

Pre-chorus 3

N.C.   **Bm7**
Because heaven sends and heaven takes,
           A   **Bm7**
Crashing cars in his brain keep him tied up to a dream.
           A
And only she can set him free, and then he says to me:

Chorus 3

D5   **F♯5**   **Bm**
"Kill me now, kill me now, kill me now, kill me   now.
D5   **F♯5**   **Bm**
  Kill me now, kill me now, kill me now, kill me   now.
    C♯5   **D5**
A - gain and a - gain."

Where The White Boys Dance

Words & Music by
Brandon Flowers, Dave Keuning, Mark Stoermer & Ronnie Vannucci

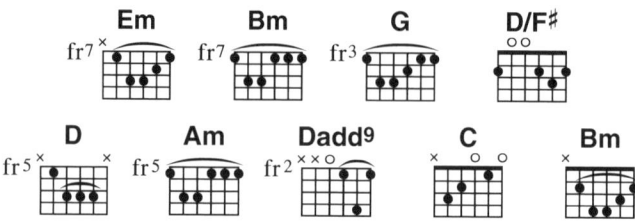

Tune guitar down a semitone

Chorus 1

N.C.
Take me to the place where the white boys dance,

Take me to the place where they run and play.

My baby is gone, you might have a chance,

Just take me to the place where the white boys dance.

Link 1

‖: Em | Em | Em | Em :‖

Verse 1

Bm   G   Bm   Em
  They hug in silence,   as the sun sets   on their empty street.
                    G   D/F♯ Em   D
Their sus - picions well they're rising high.
          Am   Dadd⁹   D Bm
And the man who sweeps them off she doesn't need.
                                      G   Bm   Em
She walks inside and,   pours a strong one,   put her mind at ease.
          G   D/F♯ Em   D
It's the calm before an - other storm,
          Am   Dadd⁹   D
And her brain shifts from the whisky to the keys.

Chorus 2

Em
Take me to the place where the white boys dance,

Take me to the place where they run and play.

My baby is gone, you might have a chance,

                                                      N.C.
Just take me to the place where the white boys dance.

Verse 2

    Bm   **G**   **Bm**
Her heart is racing,   she phones a friend and says:

            Em
"I'm in an awful place.

    G   **D/F♯**   **Em**   **D**
That fool's been messin' round on me,

     Am   **Dadd9** **D** **Bm**
I've seen it in his eyes and on his face."

                G   **Bm**
Hold on a minute,   you're talking crazy,

            Em
Don't be that jealous girl.

    G   **D/F♯**   **Em**   **D**
Just tell Levon you need an hour or two,

     Am   **Dadd9**   **D**
'Cause we're gonna go and change somebody's world.

Chorus 3

Em
Take me to the place where the white boys dance.

Take me to the place where they run and play,

My baby is gone, you might have a chance,

Just take me to the place where the white boys dance.

Solo

| **G** | **Am** | **Em** | **D** | |

| **G** | **Am** | **Em** | **D** | ‖

Bridge

           G   **Am**   **Em** **D**
It's the calm before another storm.

         Em   **D**
It's the calm before another storm,

        C   **Bm**
And her brain shifts from the whisky to the keys.

Chorus 4

Em
Take me to the place where the white boys dance,

Take me to the place where they run and play.

My baby is gone, you might have a chance,

                                        N.C.
Just take me to the place where the white boys dance.

A White Demon Love Song

Words & Music by
Brandon Flowers, Dave Keuning, Mark Stoermer & Ronnie Vannucci

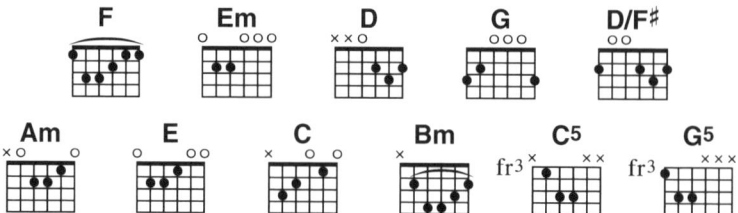

Tune guitar down a semitone

Intro   ‖: F | F | Em | Em   :‖

Verse 1
F
   White demon love song down the hall,
Em
   White demon shadow on the road.
F
   Back up your mind, there is a call,
Em   D   G
   He hears it coming after all of this time.
    D/F♯   Em
She likes the way he sings,
Am   G   F
   White demon love song's in her dreams.

Verse 2
F
   White demon, where's your selfish kiss?
Em
   White demon sorrow will arrange.
F
   Let's not forget about the fear,
Em   D   G
   Black invitation to a place that cannot change.
      D/F♯   Em F   E   Am
While   strangely ho - ly,   come   for a rain.
D
   Darling.

Chorus 1

C   Bm   Em   Am
White demon,   widen your heart's scope.

C   Bm   Em   Am
White demon,   who let your friend go?

C   Bm   Em   Am
White demon,   widen your heart's scope.

C   Bm   Em   Am
White demon,   who let your friend go?

Bridge

C5   G5
Let us be in love. (Let us be in love)

Let's do old and grey. (Let's do old and grey)

C5   G5
I won't make you cry. (I won't make you cry)

            E   Am
I will never stray. (I will never stray)

            D   Am
I will do my part. (I will do my part)

          Bm   (C)
Let us be in love to - night.

Chorus 2

C   Bm   Em   Am
White demon,   widen your heart's scope.

C   Bm   Em   Am
White demon,   who let your friend go?

C   Bm   Em   Am
White demon,   widen your heart's scope.

C   Bm   Em   Am   (C)
White demon,   who let your friend go?

Instr.

| C Bm | Em Am | D Bm | Em Am | Em Am ‖

Outro

C Bm Em Am   D   Bm
        Stand it any - more, darling,

Em Am
  Stand it.

C Bm Em   D   Bm
        I can't stand it any - more, darling,

Em Am
  Stand it. *To fade*

Who Let You Go

Words & Music by
Brandon Flowers, Dave Keuning, Mark Stoermer & Ronnie Vannucci

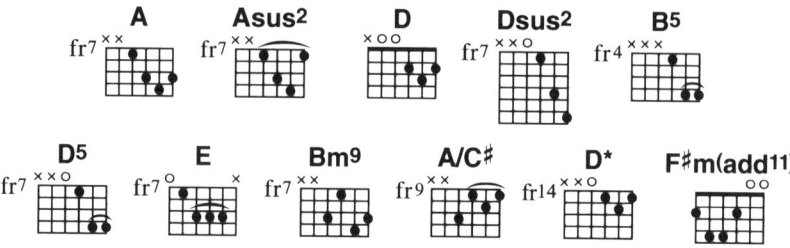

Tune guitar down a semitone

Chorus 1

    A   Asus2 A   Asus2
Who let you go?   Who let you go?

D
Who let you go?   **Dsus2**   **D**
                    Who let you go?

A   **Asus2** **A**   **Asus2**
Who let you go?   Who let you go?

D   **Dsus2**   **D**
Who let you go?   Who let you go?

Verse 1

    A   **Asus2** **A**   **Asus2**
I feel it inside,   down in my soul,

D   **Dsus2**   **D**
And I just can't hide these things I know.

A   **Asus2**
We could be friends,

      A   **Asus2**
And I promise that it won't go bad.

    D
But hopefully this story ends,

    Dsus2   **B5**
When you ain't got nothing I never had.

               D5
So let's take it slow.

Chorus 2

    A   **Asus2** **A**   **Asus2**
Who let you go?   Who let you go?

D   **Dsus2**   **D**
Who let you go?   Who let you go?

Verse 2

    A   **Asus2**
Someone must have loved you,

    A   **Asus2**
Not the way that I do.

        D
You're missing what I'm trying to say,

      Dsus2   **D**
Ain't nothing getting in my way.

     A
So tell me that's fantastic,

                    Bm9   **A/C♯ D5**
And promise me, you'll al - ways sigh.

              D*
I find it so romantic,

              B5
When you look into my beautiful eyes

        D5
And lose control.

Chorus 3

    A   **Asus2** **A**   **Asus2**
Who let you go?   Who let you go?

    D   **Dsus2**   **D**
Who let you go?   Who let you go?

    A   **Asus2** **A**   **Asus2**
Who let you go?   Who let you go?

    D   **Dsus2**   **D**
Who let you go?   Who let you go?

Bridge

     E   **D**
I don't know what it means, but I've been wondering,

    F♯m(add11)
Who let you go?

     E   **D**
And honey, when you walk my way it makes me wanna say...

Outro

    A   **Asus2** **A** **Asus2**
"Oh."

    D   **Dsus2**   **D**
Sha-la-la, sha-la-la,

     A   **Asus2** **A**   **Asus2**
𝄆: Sha-la-la,   sha-la-la,

    D   **Dsus2**   **D**
Sha-la-la, sha-la-la, la-la-la-la. :𝄇   *Repeat ad lib to fade*

Why Don't You Find Out For Yourself

Words & Music by Morrissey & Alain Whyte

Em   C   A   G   D   Am   Bm

Tune guitar down a semitone

Intro

| Em | C | A | A |

| Em | C | A | C ||

G   D
  The sanest days are mad,

                               Am
Why don't you find out for your - self?

                  C
Then you'll see the price very closely.

Link 1

| Em | C | A | A |

| Em | C | A | C ||

Verse 1

Bm   Em   C
  Some men here,

                G   Bm   Em
They have a special interest   in your ca - reer,

                  C   D   G   D
They wanna help you to grow and   then syphon all your dough.

                              Am
Why don't you find out for your - self?

                     C   G
Then you'll see the glass hidden in the grass.

                        D
You'll never believe me so,

                              Am
Why don't you find out for your - self?

              C
Sick down to my heart,

Well that's just the way it goes.

Link 2 | Em | C | A | A |

                | Em | C | A | C   ‖

Verse 2

Bm   Em   C
Some men here,

                G   Bm   Em
They know the full extent of   your distress.

          C   D   G
They kneel and pray and they   say:

                D
"Long may it last."

                             Am
Why don't you find out for your - self?

                  C   G
Then you'll see the glass hidden in the grass.

                D   Am
Back seats come and go for which you must al - low.

                C
Sick down to my heart,

Well that's just the way it goes.

Interlude | Em | C | A | A |

                | Em | C | A | C |

                | G | G | A | A |

                | C | C | D | D   ‖

Verse 3

G   D   Am
Don't rake up my mis - takes, I know exactly what they are.

                        C   G
And what do you do?   Well, you just sit there.

                        D   Am
I've been stabbed in the back so many, many times,

                    C
I don't have any skin,   but that's just the way it goes.

Outro | Em | C | A | A |

                | Em | C | A | C Am | G   ‖

Why Do I Keep Counting

Words & Music by
Brandon Flowers, Dave Keuning, Mark Stoermer & Ronnie Vannucci

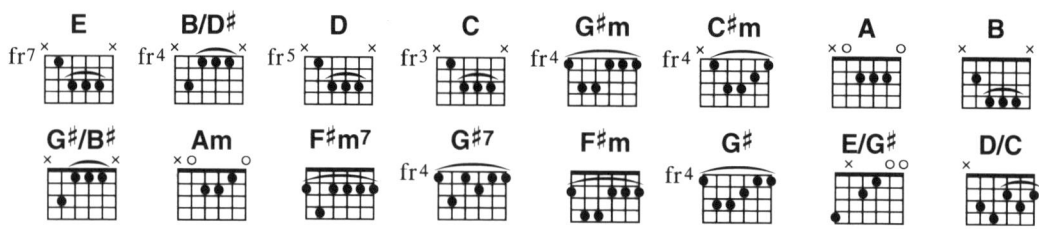

Tune guitar down a semitone

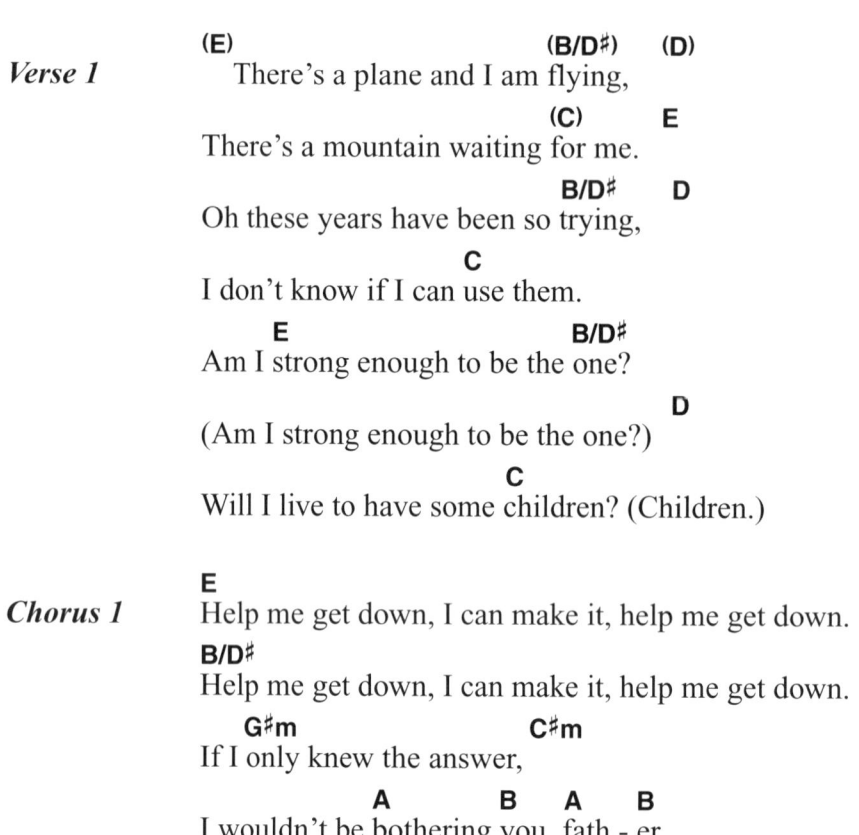

Verse 1

 (E)   (B/D♯)   (D)
    There's a plane and I am flying,

                   (C)   E
There's a mountain waiting for me.

                   B/D♯   D
Oh these years have been so trying,

             C
I don't know if I can use them.

         E   B/D♯
Am I strong enough to be the one?

                           D
(Am I strong enough to be the one?)

                C
Will I live to have some children? (Children.)

Chorus 1

     E
Help me get down, I can make it, help me get down.

B/D♯
Help me get down, I can make it, help me get down.

      G♯m   C♯m
If I only knew the answer,

           A   B   A   B
I wouldn't be bothering you, fath - er.

Chorus 2

E
Help me get down, I can make it, help me get down.
B   G♯/B♯
Help me get down, I can make it, help me get down.
    C♯m   B
If I only knew the answer,
        A   Am
And if all our days are numbered,
                         E
Then why do I keep counting?

Link

| E | E | E | E   ‖
(counting?)

Bridge 1

C♯m   A   B/D♯   G♯m
    My sugar sweet is so at - tainable,
          C♯m   F♯m   B
This be - haviour's so   unex - plainable.
      C♯m   A   B/D♯   G♯m
The days just slip and slide like they always did,
          C♯m   F♯m7   F♯m   B
The trouble is my head   won't let me forget.
G♯7   C♯m
    I took one last good look a - round,
      B   A   E/G♯   F♯m
(So many un - usual sounds,)
        G♯m   A   B
I gotta get my feet on the   ground.

Chorus 3

E
Help me get down, I can make it. (Ah.)___

Help me get down, I can make it, help me get down.
B/D♯
Help me get down, I can make it, help me get down.
    G♯m   C♯m
If I only knew the answer,
                A   B   A   B
I wouldn't be bothering you, fa - ther.

155

Chorus 4

```
E
```
Help me get down I can make it, help me get down.
```
B                              G♯/B♯
```
Help me get down I can make it, help me get down.
```
    C♯m                        B
```
If I only knew the answer,
```
        A                              Am
```
And if all our days are numbered.

Chorus 5

```
               E
```
Would you help me get down?

(I can make it, help me get down.)
```
B                              G♯/B♯
```
(Help me get down, I can make it, help me get down.)
```
    C♯m                        B
```
If I only knew the answer,
```
        E                      A
```
If I change my way of living,
```
        F♯m                    B
```
And if I pave my streets with good times,
```
        E                      A
```
Will the mountain keep on giving?
```
        C♯m      B             A     D/C
```
And if all of our days are num - bered,
```
                     C♯m       A  C  E
```
Then why do I keep counting?

The World We Live In

Words by Brandon Flowers
Music by Brandon Flowers, Dave Keuning, Mark Stoermer & Ronnie Vannucci

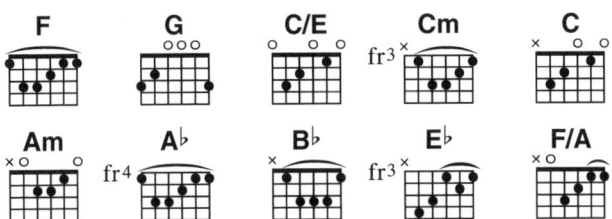

Chorus 1
N.C.   F   G
This is the world that we live in,

C/E   F
I feel myself get tired,

                      G
This is the world that we live in.

Link 1
| Cm | Cm | C | C |

Verse 1
          Cm
Well, maybe I was mistaken,

          Am   Ab
I heard a rumour that you quit this day and age,

                        C
Well, maybe I was mis - taken.

Bridge 1
F   G
Bless your body, bless your soul,

Am   Bb   C
Pray for peace and self con - trol.

Verse 2
          Cm
I got to believe it's worth it,

          Am   Ab
Without a victory, I'm so sanctified and free,

                        C
Well, maybe I'm just mis - taken.

Bridge 2

C/E B♭ C
          The lesson learned and the wheels keep turning. C/E B♭ C

Chorus 2

C/E   F   G
  This is the world that we live in,
C/E   F
I can't take blame for two.
                      G
This is the world that we live in,
     C/E   F   G Cm
And maybe we'll make it through, oh.___

Instr.

| Cm | Cm | Am | Am |

| A♭ | A♭ | C | C ‖

Bridge 3

F   G
Bless your body, bless your soul,
Am   B♭   C
Reel me in and cut my throat.
F   G
Underneath the waterfall,
Am   B♭   C   C/E
Baby we're still in this,   oh yeah.

Chorus 3

C/E   F   G
This is the world that we live in,
  C/E   F
I feel myself get tired,
                 G
This is the world that we live in.

Middle

E♭   Cm   B♭   F/A   A♭
  I had a dream that I was falling   down,
C   C/E
  There's no next time a - round.
B♭   C
A storm wastes its water on me,
        C/E B♭   C
But my life   was free.

Chorus 4

C/E   F   G
    I guess it's the world that we live in,

   C/E   F
It's not too late for that.

                                  G
This is the world that we live in,

   C/E   F
And no, we can't go back.

                                  G
This is the world that we live in,

 C/E   F
I still want something real.

                                G
This is the world that we live in,

          C/E   F   G
I know that we can heal over time.____

C/E   G C/E F
   This is the world that we live in.

G C/E   F
     This is the world that we live in.

Outro   ‖: F | G | C/E | F   :‖ *Repeat to fade*

1 2 3 4 5 6 7 8 9

159

Relative Tuning

The guitar can be tuned with the aid of pitch pipes or dedicated electronic guitar tuners which are available through your local music dealer. If you do not have a tuning device, you can use relative tuning. Estimate the pitch of the 6th string as near as possible to E or at least a comfortable pitch (not too high, as you might break other strings in tuning up). Then, while checking the various positions on the diagram, place a finger from your left hand on the:

5th fret of the E or 6th string and **tune the open A** (or 5th string) to the note (A)

5th fret of the A or 5th string and **tune the open D** (or 4th string) to the note (D)

5th fret of the D or 4th string and **tune the open G** (or 3rd string) to the note (G)

4th fret of the G or 3rd string and **tune the open B** (or 2nd string) to the note (B)

5th fret of the B or 2nd string and **tune the open E** (or 1st string) to the note (E)

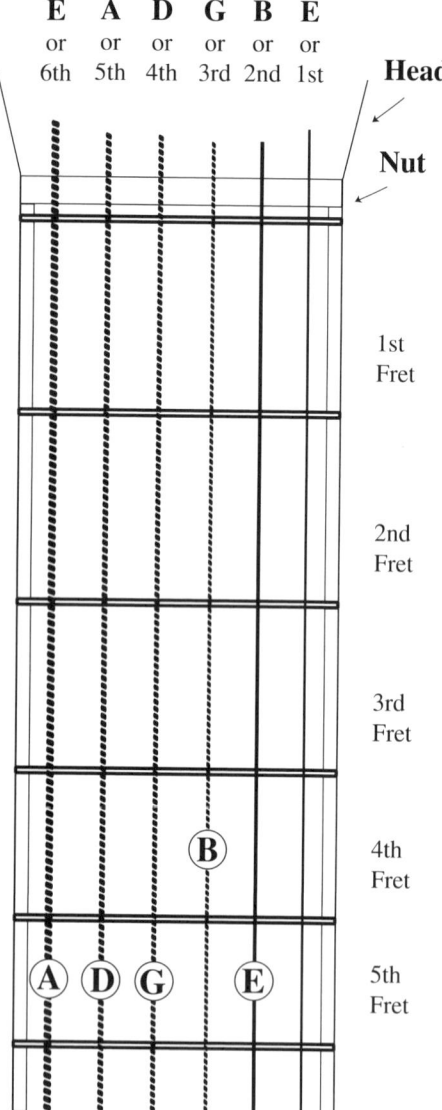

Reading Chord Boxes

Chord boxes are diagrams of the guitar neck viewed head upwards, face on as illustrated. The top horizontal line is the nut, unless a higher fret number is indicated, the others are the frets.

The vertical lines are the strings, starting from E (or 6th) on the left to E (or 1st) on the right.

The black dots indicate where to place your fingers.

Strings marked with an O are played open, not fretted. Strings marked with an X should not be played.

The curved bracket indicates a 'barre' - hold down the strings under the bracket with your first finger, using your other fingers to fret the remaining notes.

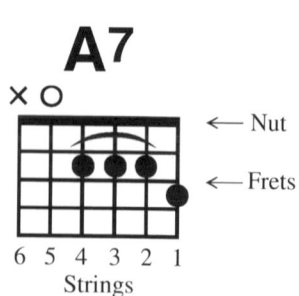